MEAT

D0701323

Of all the food available to us, red meat provides the best source of iron and zinc, two elements essential for good health. That makes meat a very important part of our diet.

Its food value is unchallenged and when trimmed of fat it is an important ingredient for most main dishes in the day's menu.

There aren't many foods that provide the versatility meat does. It can be used fresh, or frozen for later use, has many different cuts with a host of different uses, and comes in a variety of flavours for added interest.

Choose lean meat cuts, trim any fat from the meat and use low-fat cooking techniques to make the most of the nutritional advantages of eating meat.

Robyn Martin
NZ Woman's Weekly
Food Editor

CONTENTS

THE PANTRY SHELF

Unless otherwise stated, the following ingredients used in this book are:

Cream — Double, suitable for whipping

Flour — White flour, plain or standard

Sugar — White sugar

WHAT'S IN A TABLESPOON?

NEW ZEALAND
1 tablespoon =
15 mL OR 3 teaspoons
UNITED KINGDOM
1 tablespoon =
15 mL OR 3 teaspoons
AUSTRALIA
1 tablespoon =
20 mL OR 4 teaspoons
The recipes in this book were tested in Australia where a 20 mL tablespoon is standard. All measures are level.

The tablespoon in the New Zealand and United Kingdom sets of measuring spoons is 15 mL. In many recipes this difference will not matter. For recipes using baking powder, gelatine, bicarbonate of soda, small quantities of flour and cornflour, simply add another teaspoon for each tablespoon specified.

SOUPS

*Meat soups are hearty one-bowl meals – perfect
for winter days. For a complete and satisfying lunch, dinner
or supper, simply serve with crusty French bread or wholemeal
rolls. Leftovers are delicious for lunch; just heat and place in a
vacuum flask for taking to school or work.*

Basil Meatball Soup

Pea and Ham Soup

Curried Lamb Soup

Veal Dumpling Soup

*Basil Meatball Soup,
Pea and Ham Soup*

Basil Meatball Soup

1 tablespoon olive oil
2 carrots, cut into thin strips
4 cups/1 litre/1^3/$_4$ pt beef stock
125 g/4 oz vermicelli
freshly ground black pepper

BASIL MEATBALLS
250 g/8 oz lean beef mince
1 egg, lightly beaten
3 tablespoons dried breadcrumbs
2 tablespoons grated Parmesan cheese
1 tablespoon finely chopped fresh basil
or 1 teaspoon dried basil
1 tablespoon tomato sauce
3 cloves garlic, crushed
1 onion, finely chopped

1 To make meatballs, place mince, egg, breadcrumbs, Parmesan cheese, basil, tomato sauce, garlic and onion in a bowl and mix to combine. Using wet hands, roll mixture into small balls. Place meatballs on a plate lined with plastic food wrap and refrigerate for 30 minutes.

2 Heat oil in a large frying pan and cook meatballs for 10 minutes or until cooked through and browned on all sides. Add carrots and cook for 3 minutes longer.

3 Place stock in a large saucepan and bring to the boil. Add vermicelli and cook for 4-5 minutes or until vermicelli is tender. Add carrots and meatballs, season to taste with black pepper and cook for 4-5 minutes longer.

Serves 4

The meatballs for this soup are also delicious made with thyme, rosemary or parsley. Or you might like to try a mixture of herbs for something different.

Pea and Ham Soup

15 g/^{1}/$_2$ oz butter
1 tablespoon olive oil
2 cloves garlic, crushed
1 onion, finely chopped
125 g/4 oz button mushrooms, sliced
4 cups/1 litre/1^3/$_4$ pt chicken stock
^{1}/$_2$ teaspoon paprika
3 stalks celery, chopped
10 large lettuce leaves, shredded
250 g/8 oz fresh or frozen peas
125 g/4 oz diced ham
^{1}/$_4$ red pepper, finely chopped
2 tablespoons chopped fresh parsley
freshly ground black pepper

1 Heat butter and oil in a large saucepan and cook garlic, onion and mushrooms for 3 minutes. Stir in stock and paprika and bring to the boil, then reduce heat and simmer for 10 minutes.

2 Add celery, lettuce and peas and cook for 5 minutes longer or until peas are tender. Stir in ham, red pepper, parsley and black pepper to taste and cook for 3-4 minutes.

Serves 4

Serve this soup with grilled cheese triangles. Toast the required number of bread slices, cut into triangles and top with a slice of your favourite cheese and a few fresh chopped herbs. Cook under a preheated grill for 3-4 minutes or until cheese melts and browns. A sharp Cheddar cheese, goat's cheese or Gruyère are all good choices.

CURRIED LAMB SOUP

185 g/6 oz yellow split peas, washed
2 tablespoons vegetable oil
375 g/12 oz lamb shanks, cut in half
3 cloves garlic, crushed
1 onion, finely chopped
2 tablespoons curry powder
5 cups/1.2 litres/2 pt boiling water
2 tablespoons chopped fresh mint
2 carrots, diced
2 stalks celery, sliced
$^1/_2$ cup/125 mL/4 fl oz coconut milk
1 tablespoon lemon juice
freshly ground black pepper

1   Place split peas in a bowl, cover with water and set aside to soak for 10 minutes.

2   Heat oil in a large saucepan and cook lamb shanks for 5-6 minutes or until browned on all sides. Add garlic, onion and curry powder and cook, stirring, for 5 minutes longer. Drain peas and add peas and boiling water to pan. Bring soup to the boil, skimming off any scum from the surface, then reduce heat and simmer for 1 hour.

3   Remove shanks from soup and set aside to cool. Remove meat from bones and cut into even-sized pieces. Remove peas from soup and place in a food processor or blender and process until smooth. Return pea purée and meat to pan, then stir in mint and carrots and cook for 5 minutes. Add celery, coconut milk, lemon juice and black pepper to taste and cook over a medium heat without boiling for 3-5 minutes.

Serves 6

Economically, a hearty meat soup is a good choice, because usually a less tender and therefore less expensive cut of meat is used. A meat soup generally uses less meat than other dishes and so is a good choice for those trying to reduce their intake of red meat.

Veal Dumpling Soup

60 g/2 oz butter
2 onions, chopped
4 rashers bacon, chopped
500 g/1 lb lean veal, cut into thin strips
$^1/_2$ cup/60 g/2 oz flour, sifted
1 tablespoon paprika
8 cups/2 litres/3$^1/_2$ pt beef stock
2 red peppers, halved, roasted, skinned
and chopped
4 tablespoons tomato paste (purée)
1 tablespoon caraway seeds
freshly ground black pepper
2 tablespoons finely chopped fresh
coriander or parsley

HERB DUMPLINGS
2 cups/250 g/8 oz self-raising
flour, sifted
60 g/2 oz butter, cut into small pieces
2 eggs, lightly beaten
$^1/_3$ cup/90 mL/3 fl oz milk
2 tablespoons chopped fresh herbs, such
as parsley, coriander, rosemary or thyme

Serves 6

A hearty soup that is a meal in itself. You may wish to use beef in place of the veal.

1   Melt butter in a large saucepan and cook onions and bacon over a medium heat for 4-5 minutes or until bacon is crisp. Using a slotted spoon remove onions and bacon from pan and drain on absorbent kitchen paper.

2   Add veal to pan in small batches and cook until brown on all sides. Remove from pan and drain on absorbent kitchen paper.

3   Combine flour and paprika, stir into pan and cook for 1 minute. Remove pan from heat and gradually blend in stock. Return onion mixture and meat to pan, bring to the boil, then reduce heat and simmer for 1$^1/_2$ hours or until meat is tender. Add red peppers, tomato paste (purée) and caraway seeds and simmer for 15 minutes longer. Season to taste with black pepper.

4   To make dumplings, place flour and butter in a food processor and process until mixture resembles coarse bread crumbs. Place eggs, milk and herbs in a small bowl and mix to combine. With machine running, pour egg mixture into flour mixture and process to a smooth dough. Turn dough onto a lightly floured surface and knead quickly. Shape tablespoons of mixture into small balls and cook in boiling water in a large saucepan for 10-12 minutes or until they rise to the surface. Remove dumplings using a slotted spoon. To serve, place a few dumplings in each soup bowl, ladle soup over and sprinkle with coriander or parsley.

To roast peppers, halve, remove seeds, place them under a hot grill (skin side up) and cook until the skin blisters and chars. Place in a paper or plastic food bag and leave for 10 minutes or until cool enough to handle. The skins will then slip off.

Left: Curried Lamb Soup

STARTERS

*Whether it's a family meal or a special occasion,
serving meat as a first course or starter is another way in which
you can reduce the amount of meat in your diet. For a balanced
meal, follow a meat starter with a vegetable main course.*

Smoked Beef Salad

Smoked Beef Salad

125 g/4 oz alfalfa sprouts
8 thin slices cold smoked beef or
rare roast beef
440 g/14 oz canned artichoke hearts,
drained and halved
1/4 red pepper, cut into thin strips

RED WINE VINEGAR DRESSING
1/4 cup/60 mL/2 fl oz olive oil
1/4 cup/60 mL/2 fl oz red wine vinegar
1 tablespoon finely chopped
fresh parsley
freshly ground black pepper

1   Place alfalfa sprouts on a large serving platter. Roll up each slice of beef and arrange decoratively on sprouts. Place artichoke hearts between each roll and pile red pepper strips in centre of plate.

2   To make dressing, place oil, vinegar, parsley and black pepper to taste in a screwtop jar and shake well to combine. Just prior to serving, drizzle dressing over salad.

Serves 4

This salad also makes a delicious luncheon when served with crusty bread and a salad of tomatoes sprinkled with chopped fresh basil and balsamic vinegar.

Honeyed Spareribs

16 pork spareribs, trimmed of visible fat
1 1/2 cups/375 mL/12 fl oz rice
wine vinegar
1/2 cup/125 mL/4 fl oz soy sauce
1/2 cup/170 g/5 1/2 oz honey
4 small fresh red chillies, seeds
removed and chopped
2 spring onions, chopped
4 cloves garlic, crushed
1 tablespoon grated fresh ginger

HONEY SAUCE
2 onions, chopped
1 cup/250 mL/8 fl oz chicken stock
2 tablespoons lemon juice
2 tablespoons chopped fresh parsley
60 g/2 oz butter, melted

1   Place spareribs in a large stainless steel, ceramic or glass bowl or baking dish. Place vinegar, soy sauce, honey, chillies, spring onions, garlic and ginger in a bowl and mix to combine. Pour over spareribs, cover and refrigerate for at least 4 hours or overnight.

2   Drain ribs and reserve marinade. Cook ribs on a preheated barbecue, brushing occasionally with some of the reserved marinade, for 15-20 minutes or until golden and tender.

3   To make sauce, place remaining reserved marinade, onions, stock, lemon juice and parsley in a saucepan. Bring to the boil, reduce heat and cook, uncovered, for 15 minutes or until sauce is reduced by half. Place sauce in a food processor or blender and, with machine running, pour in hot melted butter and process to combine. Pour sauce over hot ribs or pass around separately.

Serves 8

The ideal starter for a barbecue party, these ribs need to be served with a pile of paper napkins for easy eating.

COUNTRY TERRINE

Oven temperature
180°C, 350°F, Gas 4

750 g/1$^{1}/_2$ lb pork and veal mince
1 onion, finely chopped
2 cloves garlic, crushed
4 spinach leaves, shredded
10 pitted prunes, roughly chopped
1 large green apple, finely diced
60 g/2 oz pine nuts
$^{1}/_4$ cup/60 mL/2 fl oz brandy
$^{1}/_4$ cup/30 g/1 oz flour
$^{1}/_2$ cup/125 mL/4 fl oz cream (double)
2 teaspoons chopped fresh parsley
freshly ground black pepper
500 g/1 lb bacon rashers

1 Place mince, onion, garlic, spinach, prunes, apple, pine nuts, brandy, flour, cream, parsley and black pepper to taste in a large bowl and mix to combine.

2 Line a lightly greased 11 x 21 cm/ 4$^{1}/_2$ x 8$^{1}/_2$ in loaf tin with bacon rashers allowing slices to overhang the top. Pack mince mixture into loaf tin and smooth top. Fold overhanging rashers into the centre to cover filling. Cover tin tightly with a double thickness of aluminium foil. Place in a baking dish with enough hot water to come halfway up sides of tin and cook for 1$^{1}/_2$ hours or until mixture is coming away from sides of tin and is cooked through.

This terrine is also excellent as a lunch or picnic dish when served with crusty French bread and mango chutney.

Serves 10

3 Remove foil, drain off excess liquid and refrigerate overnight.

FRUITY PORK ROULADE

4 lean butterfly pork steaks
2 cups/500 mL/16 fl oz beef stock
4 stalks celery, chopped
2 onions, chopped

FRUIT FILLING
60 g/2 oz pine nuts
100 g/3$^{1}/_2$ oz pitted prunes
60 g/2 oz dried apricots
1 tablespoon grated fresh ginger
1 teaspoon chopped fresh sage
3 tablespoons fruit chutney
4 rashers bacon, chopped
3 tablespoons brandy
freshly ground black pepper

1 To make filling, place pine nuts, prunes, apricots, ginger, sage, chutney, bacon, brandy and black pepper to taste in a food processor and process until finely chopped.

2 Open out steaks and pound to about 5 mm/$^{1}/_4$ in thick. Spread filling over steaks and roll up tightly. Secure each roll with string.

Perfect finger food to serve with pre-dinner drinks. Served on a bed of mixed lettuces, these pork slices also make an elegant starter.

3 Place stock, celery and onions in a large saucepan and bring to the boil. Add pork rolls, cover and simmer for 20 minutes or until pork is cooked. Transfer pork rolls to a plate, set aside to cool, then cover and refrigerate for 2-3 hours. To serve, cut each roll into slices.

Serves 6

Country Terrine

CURRIED SAUSAGE PUFFS

Oven temperature
200°C, 400°F, Gas 6

Sausage meat wrapped in pastry is always a favourite finger food. These curry-flavoured puffs are sure to be a hit and are ideal for entertaining as they can be made and cooked ahead of time then just reheated when required. They also freeze well and can be reheated straight from frozen.

185 g/6 oz prepared puff pastry

CURRIED FILLING
375 g/12 oz sausage meat
1 small carrot, grated
2 spring onions, chopped
1 tablespoon fruit chutney
1 teaspoon curry powder
freshly ground black pepper

1   To make filling, place sausage meat, carrot, onions, chutney, curry powder and black pepper to taste in a bowl and mix to combine.

2   Roll out pastry to 3 mm/^{1}/$_8$ in thickness and cut into two strips, each 10 x 25 cm/4 x 10 in. Place half the filling along centre of each pastry strip and roll up from the long side. Brush edge of pastry with water to seal. Cut roll into 1 cm/^{1}/$_2$ in slices.

3   Place slices on lightly greased baking trays and bake for 15 minutes or until puffed and golden.

Makes 24

Below left: Curried Sausage Puffs
Below: Chilli Bean Cups

CHILLI BEAN CUPS

2 tablespoons vegetable oil
1 large onion, chopped
2 cloves garlic, crushed
250 g/8 oz lean beef mince
2 teaspoons chilli powder
2 teaspoons ground cumin
440 g/14 oz canned tomatoes,
undrained and mashed
440 g/14 oz canned red kidney
beans, drained
freshly ground black pepper

POLENTA PASTRY
185 g/6 oz butter
185 g/6 oz cream cheese
2 cups/250 g/8 oz flour, sifted
1 cup/170 g/5^{1}/$_{2}$ oz polenta (corn meal)

Makes 24

1   To make pastry, place butter and cream cheese in a food processor and process to combine. Add flour and polenta (corn meal) and process to form a soft dough. Turn dough onto a lightly floured surface and knead until smooth. Divide dough into small balls and press into lightly greased muffin pans. Bake for 20 minutes or until golden brown.

2   Heat oil in a large frying pan and cook onion for 3-4 minutes or until soft. Add garlic, mince, chilli powder and cumin, and cook for 4-5 minutes longer. Stir in tomatoes and beans, bring to the boil, then reduce heat and simmer, uncovered, for 1 hour or until most of the liquid has evaporated and the mixture is quite dry. Season to taste with black pepper and spoon into hot polenta cups. Serve immediately.

Oven temperature
180°C, 350°F, Gas 4

The polenta cups and the meat mixture can be made ahead of time and reheated just before serving. The polenta cups will keep for up to a week in an airtight container or for several months in the freezer.

SALADS

Succulent strips or slices of meat tossed or drizzled with a tangy dressing are the basis of these meat salads. Perfect as light meals, these salads are substantial enough to satisfy the hungriest diners.

Beef and Basil Salad

Beef and Basil Salad

4 eye fillet steaks, each 2.5 cm/1 in
thick, trimmed of all visible fat
4 tablespoons vegetable oil
12 baby eggplant (aubergines), cut into
slices, lengthwise
185 g/6 oz sugar snap peas
1 bunch rocket or 1 lettuce, leaves
separated and washed
4 tomatoes, cut into wedges

BASIL DRESSING
1 large bunch basil
$^1/_2$ cup/125 mL/4 fl oz olive oil
$^1/_4$ cup/60 mL/2 fl oz tarragon vinegar
2 cloves garlic, crushed
freshly ground black pepper

Serves 8

1   Cook steaks under a preheated grill for 3 minutes each side. Set aside to cool, then cut into thin strips.

2   Heat oil in a large frying pan and cook eggplant (aubergines) over a medium heat until brown. Remove from pan and drain on absorbent kitchen paper. Blanch peas in boiling water for 2-3 minutes or until they just change colour. Drain, then refresh under cold running water.

3   Arrange rocket or lettuce leaves, steak, eggplant (aubergines), peas and tomatoes attractively on a large serving platter.

4   To make dressing, place basil leaves, oil, vinegar, garlic and black pepper to taste in a food processor or blender and process until smooth. Spoon dressing over salad.

Served with crusty bread rolls, this salad is a meal in itself.

Warm Veal and Lemon Salad

2 tablespoons vegetable oil
375 g/12 oz thin veal schnitzels
(escalopes), cut into strips
1 onion, sliced
1 red pepper, cut into thin strips
1 tablespoon honey
1 tablespoon brown sugar
$^1/_4$ cup/60 mL/2 fl oz white wine
$^1/_4$ cup/60 mL/2 fl oz lemon juice
315 g/10 oz canned baby sweet corn,
drained
125 g/4 oz snow peas (mangetout),
topped and tailed
1 tablespoon chopped fresh dill

Serves 4

1   Heat oil in a large frying pan and stir-fry veal, onion and red pepper over a medium heat for 3 minutes or until veal is cooked. Using a slotted spoon, remove veal and vegetables from pan and set aside.

2   Stir honey, sugar, wine and lemon juice into pan juices and cook for 3 minutes.

3   Add sweet corn, snow peas (mangetout) and dill and stir-fry for 2 minutes or until snow peas (mangetout) just change colour. Return veal mixture to pan and stir-fry for 2 minutes longer or until heated through.

When there's a chill in the air, a warm salad makes the perfect meal. This salad is also delicious made with lamb or beef in place of the veal.

OPEN BEEF SALAD SANDWICHES

When you want to serve something a little more substantial with drinks, these sandwiches are the answer. They should be made as close to serving time as possible. Remember the mayonnaise needs to be made ahead of time leaving only the assembly of the sandwiches to be done at the last minute.

1 loaf crusty French bread, cut
into thick slices
1 lettuce, leaves separated and washed
500 g/1 lb cold rare roast beef slices

TARRAGON MAYONNAISE
4 egg yolks
1 tablespoon white vinegar
1 tablespoon chopped fresh tarragon or
2 teaspoons dried tarragon
250 g/8 oz butter
1 teaspoon canned green peppercorns,
drained

1   To make mayonnaise, place egg yolks, vinegar and tarragon in a food processor or blender and process until light and fluffy. Melt butter until it is hot and bubbling. With machine running, slowly pour in melted butter and process until mayonnaise thickens. Transfer to a small bowl and stir in peppercorns. Cover and chill.

2   Top each bread slice with a lettuce leaf, several beef slices and a spoonful of mayonnaise. Serve immediately.

Makes 10

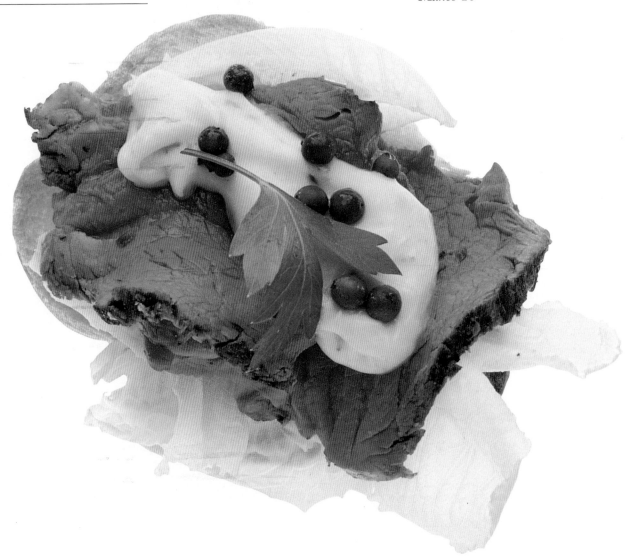

Open Beef Salad Sandwiches

CARPACCIO

500 g/1 lb eye fillet beef, in one piece
1 lettuce, leaves separated and washed
1 bunch /250 g/8 oz watercress
90 g/3 oz Parmesan cheese, grated

MUSTARD MAYONNAISE
1 egg
1 tablespoon lemon juice
2 cloves garlic, crushed
2 teaspoons Dijon mustard
$^1/_2$ cup/125 mL/4 fl oz olive oil
freshly ground black pepper

1   Trim meat of all visible fat and cut into wafer-thin slices. Arrange beef slices, lettuce leaves and watercress attractively on four serving plates. Sprinkle with Parmesan cheese.

2   To make mayonnaise, place egg, lemon juice, garlic and mustard in a food processor or blender and process to combine. With machine running, slowly add oil and continue processing until mayonnaise thickens. Season to taste with black pepper. Spoon a little mayonnaise over salad and serve immediately.

Serves 4

To achieve very thin slices of beef, wrap the fillet in plastic food wrap and place in the freezer for 15 minutes or until firm, then slice using a very sharp knife.

MAIN MEALS

In this chapter you will find dishes to suit all occasions. Cassoulet is perfect for a casual gathering of friends, while Beef with Wine Sauce is just the right dish for last-minute entertaining. Many of the recipes serve six or eight, making them ideal for larger gatherings. Or you can freeze half to have on hand for a quick meal.

Beef in Red Wine

BEEF IN RED WINE

155 g/5 oz bacon, cut into strips
1 tablespoon vegetable oil
1 kg/2 lb chuck steak, cut into
2.5 cm/1 in cubes
2 carrots, sliced
1 onion, sliced
^{1}/4 cup/30 g/1 oz flour
freshly ground black pepper
1^1/2 cups/375 mL/12 fl oz red wine
1 cup/250 mL/8 fl oz beef stock
2 tablespoons tomato paste (purée)
2 cloves garlic, crushed
1 teaspoon dried thyme
1 bay leaf
30 g/1 oz butter
18 small onions
18 button mushrooms

Serves 6

1   Place bacon in a large flameproof casserole and cook for 2 minutes. Remove bacon and drain on absorbent kitchen paper. Add oil to casserole and cook beef in batches for 4-5 minutes or until browned. Remove and set aside. Add carrots and sliced onion and cook for 4-5 minutes.

2   Drain excess fat from casserole and return bacon and meat to dish. Add flour and black pepper to taste, toss to combine and cook for 2 minutes longer. Stir in wine, stock, tomato paste (purée), garlic, thyme and bay leaf, bring to the boil, then transfer to a preheated oven and cook for 1^1/2 hours.

3   Melt butter in a large frying pan and cook small onions over a medium heat for 10 minutes. Remove, add to casserole and cook for 30 minutes longer. Add mushrooms to pan and cook for 3-4 minutes. Stir into casserole.

Oven temperature
150°C, 300°F, Gas 2

Lean meat plays an important part in a balanced diet. Lean beef, lamb and pork are highly nutritious. A 125 g/4 oz cooked serve provides much of the daily requirement of protein, the B-group vitamins, iron and zinc.

OSSO BUCCO

1 tablespoon olive oil
2 red peppers, cut into strips
2 onions, chopped
4 thick slices shin veal on the bone
^{1}/2 cup/60 g/2 oz flour
30 g/1 oz butter
^{1}/2 cup/125 mL/4 fl oz dry white wine
^{1}/2 cup/125 mL/4 fl oz chicken stock
440 g/14 oz canned tomatoes, undrained and mashed
freshly ground black pepper
1 tablespoon chopped fresh parsley

Serves 4

1   Heat oil in a large frying pan and cook red peppers and onions over a medium heat for 10 minutes or until onions are transparent. Using a slotted spoon, remove onion mixture and set aside. Toss veal in flour and shake off excess. Add butter to frying pan and cook until butter foams. Add veal and cook for 4-5 minutes each side or until browned.

2   Stir in wine and stock and bring to the boil, stirring to lift sediment from base of pan. Boil until liquid is reduced by half. Add tomatoes and return onion mixture to pan, cover and simmer for 1 hour or until meat falls away from the bone. Season to taste with black pepper and sprinkle with parsley.

The name of this dish means 'hollow bones' and is a specialty from the Italian town of Milan.

SPICY BRAISED BEEF

2 kg/4 lb blade steak, in one piece
$^1/_2$ cup/60 g/2 oz flour
30 g/1 oz ghee or clarified butter
3 onions, chopped
3 cloves garlic, crushed
1 tablespoon grated fresh ginger
1 teaspoon finely grated lemon rind
3 tablespoons curry powder
1 cup/250 mL/8 fl oz tamarind liquid
500 g/1 lb natural yogurt
$^1/_2$ cup/45 g/1$^1/_2$ oz desiccated coconut
1 cup/250 mL/8 fl oz coconut milk

RED DHAL
1 cup/200 g/6$^1/_2$ oz red lentils, washed
2 cups/500 mL/16 fl oz water
1 stick cinnamon
3 whole cloves
1 teaspoon black peppercorns, cracked
30 g/1 oz ghee or clarified butter
2 onions, sliced
1 teaspoon ground coriander
1 teaspoon ground cumin
1 teaspoon ground cardamom
1 teaspoon chilli paste (sambal oelek)
3 cloves garlic, crushed
1 cup/90 g/3 oz desiccated coconut

Tamarind is the large pod of the tamarind or Indian date tree. After picking, it is seeded and peeled then pressed into a dark brown pulp.
To make tamarind liquid, mix tamarind with warm water then use in chutneys, sauces, curries or recipes such as this one. Tamarind is available from Asian food shops.
If tamarind is unavailable use 1 cup/250 mL/8 fl oz beef stock in place of the tamarind liquid. The taste will be different but still delicious.

1   Toss beef in flour and shake off excess. Melt ghee or butter in a large saucepan and cook beef over a high heat until browned on all sides. Add onions, garlic, ginger, lemon rind, curry powder, tamarind liquid, yogurt and coconut to pan, cover and simmer for 1$^1/_2$-2 hours or until meat is tender. Stir in coconut milk and simmer for 15 minutes longer.

2   To make dhal, place lentils, water, cinnamon, cloves and peppercorns in a large saucepan and bring to the boil, then reduce heat and simmer for 30 minutes or until lentils are cooked. Remove cinnamon and cloves and discard.

3   Melt ghee or butter in a frying pan and cook onions, coriander, cumin, cardamom, chilli paste (sambal oelek), garlic and coconut over medium heat for 4-5 minutes or until onion is golden. Stir onion mixture into lentil mixture.

4   Remove beef from cooking liquid and set aside to rest in a warm place for 15 minutes. Return pan to heat, bring liquid to the boil and boil rapidly for 5-10 minutes or until liquid thickens. Serve beef cut into slices with gravy and accompany with dhal.

Serves 8

'Tamarind is the large pod of the Indian tamarind tree.
It is usually mixed with warm water to make tamarind juice or liquid'

Spicy Braised Beef

SPICY SAUSAGE HOTPOT

200 g/6^1/$_2$ oz dried black-eyed beans
3 cloves garlic, crushed
1 bay leaf
2 teaspoons ground cinnamon
^{1}/$_4$ teaspoon ground nutmeg
6 pork sausages
15 g/^{1}/$_2$ oz butter
125 g/4 oz thinly sliced pepperoni salami
3 tablespoons chopped fresh parsley

For a speedy version of this recipe you could use 440 g/ 14 oz canned beans, in which case you can omit the first step.
All that this hotpot needs to make a complete meal is a tossed green salad and crusty wholemeal bread.

1 Place beans in a large bowl, cover with water and set aside to soak overnight. Drain beans and place with garlic, bay leaf, cinnamon and nutmeg in a saucepan with enough water to cover. Bring to the boil and boil for 10 minutes, then reduce heat and simmer for 45-60 minutes or until beans are cooked. Drain and set aside.

2 Cook sausages under a preheated grill for 5-7 minutes each side or until cooked through. Slice sausages and set aside.

3 Melt butter in a large frying pan and cook salami over a medium heat for 5 minutes or until crisp. Add sausages and beans to pan and cook for 5 minutes longer or until the mixture is heated through. Sprinkle with parsley and serve.

Serves 6

Left: Spicy Sausage Hotpot
Below: Veal with Wine Sauce

VEAL WITH WINE SAUCE

8 veal schnitzels (escalopes)
$^1/_4$ cup/30 g/1 oz flour
60 g/2 oz butter
$^1/_2$ cup/125 mL/4 fl oz lemon juice
$^1/_2$ cup/125 mL/4 fl oz white wine
1 lemon, cut into thin slices

1   Toss veal in flour, then shake off excess flour.

2   Melt butter in a large frying pan and, when bubbling, add veal and cook for 1-2 minutes each side. Sprinkle with lemon juice, remove from pan and set aside to keep warm.

3   Add wine to pan, bring to the boil over a high heat and boil, stirring constantly, until liquid is reduced to $^1/_4$ cup/60 mL/2 fl oz. Spoon sauce over veal, top with lemon slices and serve immediately.

Serves 4

Veal schnitzels (escalopes) take only minutes to cook. Take care that you do not overcook them or they will be tough.

Above: Apple Pork Casserole
Right: Cassoulet

APPLE PORK CASSEROLE

30 g/1 oz butter
2 onions, chopped
500 g/1 lb lean diced pork
3 large apples, peeled, cored
and chopped
1 tablespoon dried mixed herbs
3 cups/750 mL/1¹/4 pt chicken stock
freshly ground black pepper

APPLE SAUCE
30 g/1 oz butter
2 apples, peeled, cored and chopped
2 tablespoons snipped fresh chives
440 g/14 oz canned tomatoes, undrained
and mashed
1 teaspoon cracked black peppercorns

Serves 4

This recipe is also delicious made using lean diced lamb in place of the pork. Serve with boiled brown or white rice and a green vegetable such as cabbage or beans.

1   Heat butter in a large frying pan and cook onions and pork over a medium heat for 5 minutes. Add apples, herbs, stock and black pepper to taste, bring to the boil, then reduce heat and simmer for 1 hour or until pork is tender. Using a slotted spoon remove pork and set aside.

2   Push liquid and solids through a sieve and return to pan with pork.

3   To make sauce, melt butter in a frying pan and cook apple over a medium heat for 2 minutes. Stir in chives and tomatoes and bring to the boil, reduce heat and simmer for 5 minutes. Pour into pan with pork and cook over a medium heat for 5 minutes longer. Just prior to serving, sprinkle with cracked black peppercorns.

CASSOULET

2 tablespoons olive oil
90 g/3 oz bacon, chopped
2 onions, chopped
4 cloves garlic, crushed
500 g/1 lb lean pork, cut into
5 cm/2 in pieces
500 g/1 lb lean lamb, cut into
5 cm/2 in pieces
500 g/1 lb thick pork sausages
500 g/1 lb canned lima beans
2 x 440 g/14 oz canned tomato purée
4 tomatoes, peeled and chopped
2 tablespoons chopped fresh sage or
2 teaspoons dried sage
2 tablespoons chopped fresh thyme or
2 teaspoons dried thyme
1 cup/250 mL/8 fl oz beef stock
1 cup/250 mL/8 fl oz red wine
freshly ground black pepper

1   Heat 1 tablespoon oil in a large frying pan and cook bacon, onions and garlic for 4-5 minutes or until onions are soft. Transfer to a large casserole.

2   Heat remaining oil in frying pan and cook pork and lamb in batches over a high heat for 4-5 minutes or until browned on all sides. Transfer to casserole. Add sausages to frying pan and cook for 4-5 minutes or until browned on all sides. Remove, cut each sausage into three and add to casserole.

3   Stir beans, tomato purée, tomatoes, sage, thyme, stock and wine into casserole and bake for 1$\frac{1}{2}$-2 hours or until meat is tender. Season to taste with black pepper and serve.

Serves 10

Oven temperature
150°C, 300°F, Gas 2

This version of the traditional dish is great for feeding a crowd. Its name comes from the special earthenware dish that was originally used to cook it in – a cassolo.

CORIANDER SHANKS

Oven temperature
150°C, 300°F, Gas 2

Lamb shanks are an economical cut that make a tasty and satisfying family meal. The secret to a good lamb shank casserole is long slow cooking; the meat should fall from the bone. This dish is delicious served with jacket baked potatoes and boiled or steamed cabbage. The potatoes can cook in the oven with the casserole and will take 1-1 1/2 hours.

1 tablespoon olive oil
4 lamb shanks
1 onion, sliced
1 carrot, sliced
440 g/14 oz canned tomatoes, undrained and mashed
1 teaspoon ground allspice
1/2 teaspoon ground cumin
1/2 teaspoon ground coriander
2 teaspoons paprika
1 teaspoon finely grated lemon rind
1 cup/250 mL/8 fl oz beef stock
2 tablespoons lemon juice
2 tablespoons chopped fresh coriander

1 Heat oil in a large frying pan and cook shanks over a high heat for 5 minutes or until brown on all sides. Transfer to a large flameproof casserole dish.

2 Add onion and carrot to pan and cook for 5 minutes or until onion is soft. Transfer to casserole dish. Stir in tomatoes, allspice, cumin, coriander, paprika, lemon rind and stock, then cover and bake for 1 1/2-2 hours or until meat is tender.

3 Remove shanks from casserole, stir in lemon juice and cook over high heat until sauce reduces and thickens. Return shanks to sauce and sprinkle with coriander.

Serves 4

BEEF WITH WINE SAUCE

750 g/1¹/₂ lb eye fillet beef, in one piece
30 g/1 oz butter
1 onion, chopped
1 clove garlic, crushed
1 carrot, chopped
1 stalk celery, chopped
1 cup/250 mL/8 fl oz beef stock
¹/₄ cup/60 mL/2 fl oz red wine
3 tablespoons tomato paste (purée)
freshly ground black pepper

1   Tie fillet with string to hold in shape. Melt butter in a large frying pan and cook fillet over a high heat until browned on all sides. Transfer to a baking dish and cook for 30 minutes or until cooked to your liking.

2   Add onion, garlic, carrot and celery to frying pan and cook, stirring constantly, for 5 minutes. Stir in stock, wine and tomato paste (purée), bring to the boil, then reduce heat and simmer for 5 minutes or until sauce reduces and thickens slightly. Season to taste with black pepper.

3   To serve, slice meat and arrange on a serving platter, then spoon over sauce.

Serves 4

Oven temperature
200°C, 400°F, Gas 6

Perfect for mid-week entertaining, this dish takes little time to cook and is always sure to impress. Serve with creamy mashed potatoes and steamed or boiled green beans or zucchini (courgettes).

INDIAN SHEPHERD'S PIE

Oven temperature
180°C, 350°F, Gas 4

Similar to the African dish
known as Babotie, this
shepherd's pie is delicious
served with boiled or
steamed white or brown rice,
a fresh tomato salad and a
bowl of fruit chutney.
For a more traditional
shepherd's pie omit the
custard topping and top with
mashed potato and grated
cheese.

1 cup/60 g/2 oz breadcrumbs, made
from stale bread
750 g/1^1/2 lb lean lamb mince
2 onions, chopped
2 apples, cored and chopped
90 g/3 oz dried figs, chopped
90 g/3 oz sultanas
60 g/2 oz slivered almonds
^{1}/4 cup/60 mL/2 fl oz lemon juice
4 tablespoons fruit chutney
freshly ground black pepper

CUSTARD TOPPING
1 cup/250 mL/8 fl oz milk
2 eggs
^{1}/2 teaspoon ground nutmeg

1   Place breadcrumbs, mince, onions,
apples, figs, sultanas, almonds, lemon
juice, chutney and black pepper to taste
in a bowl and mix to combine. Spoon
meat mixture into a greased 4 cup/1 litre/
1^3/4 pt capacity ovenproof dish and bake
for 10 minutes.

2   To make topping, place milk, eggs and
nutmeg in a bowl and whisk to combine.
Pour over meat mixture and bake for 30
minutes longer or until custard is set and
meat is cooked.

Serves 6

CARDAMOM LAMB

Oven temperature
150°C, 300°F, Gas 2

Coconut milk can be
purchased in a number of
forms: canned, or as a long-
life product in cartons, or as a
powder to which you add
water. Once opened it has a
short life and should be used
within a day or so. It is
available from Asian food
stores and some
supermarkets.

2 tablespoons vegetable oil
3 carrots, sliced
3 onions, sliced
750 g/1^1/2 lb lean diced lamb
1 tablespoon flour
1 bay leaf, crumbled
1 teaspoon ground cardamom
2 teaspoons ground cumin
1 teaspoon chilli paste (sambal oelek)
1 cup/250 mL/8 fl oz coconut milk
freshly ground black pepper

1   Heat oil in a large frying pan and cook
carrots and onions over a medium heat
for 5 minutes or until onions are soft.
Transfer to a large casserole dish.

2   Toss lamb in flour and shake off
excess. Add meat to pan and cook over a
high heat for 5 minutes or until browned
on all sides. Transfer meat to casserole
dish.

3   Add bay leaf, cardamom, cumin, chilli
paste (sambal oelek) and coconut milk to
casserole and mix to combine. Bake for
1^1/2-2 hours or until meat is tender.
Season to taste with black pepper.

Serves 4

Indian Shepherd's Pie
Cardamom Lamb

MEXICAN MEATLOAF

Oven temperature
180°C, 350°F, Gas 4

To cook this meatloaf in the microwave, mix as described in the recipe, then press half the meat mixture into a lightly greased 11 x 21 cm/4^1/$_2$ x 8^1/$_2$ in microwave-safe loaf container. Top with half the grated cheese, then cover with remaining meat mixture. Cook on MEDIUM-HIGH (70%) for 15 minutes. Drain off any liquid and stand for 10 minutes. Turn meatloaf onto a microwave-safe plate, top and cook on HIGH (100%) for 3 minutes or until cheese melts.

500 g/1 lb lean lamb or beef mince
2 tablespoons or 30 g/1 oz packet taco seasoning mix
1 egg
1 cup/60 g/2 oz breadcrumbs, made from stale bread
125 g/4 oz tasty cheese (mature Cheddar), grated
1 cup/250 mL/8 fl oz taco sauce
30 g/1 oz corn chips

1   Place mince, taco seasoning mix, egg and breadcrumbs in a bowl and mix to combine. Press half the mince mixture into a lightly greased 11 x 21 cm/4^1/$_2$ x 8^1/$_2$ in loaf tin. Top with half the grated cheese, then cover with remaining meat mixture. Bake for 40 minutes, then drain off any liquid, cover and set aside to stand for 10 minutes.

2   Turn meatloaf onto an ovenproof plate, brush with taco sauce and top with corn chips and remaining cheese. Bake at 200°C/400°F/Gas 6 for 10 minutes or until cheese is melted. Serve hot, warm or cold.

Serves 4

28

Left: Mexican Meatloaf
Above: Roast Pork Loin

ROAST PORK LOIN

1.5 kg/3 lb boneless pork loin
1 tablespoon coarse cooking salt

SPINACH STUFFING
30 g/1 oz butter
4 spinach leaves, stalks removed and leaves shredded
3 tablespoons pine nuts
¹/₂ cup/30 g/1 oz breadcrumbs, made from stale bread
¹/₄ teaspoon ground nutmeg
freshly ground black pepper

CHUNKY APPLE RELISH
1 small green apple, peeled, cored and sliced
1 small pear, peeled, cored and sliced
2 teaspoons chopped dried dates
4 tablespoons apple juice
2 teaspoons honey
1 teaspoon finely grated lemon rind
pinch ground cloves

Serves 8

1   Unroll loin and make a cut in the middle of the fleshy part of the meat, making a space for the stuffing. Score the rind with a sharp knife, cutting down into the fat under the rind.

2   To make stuffing, melt butter in a frying pan and cook spinach and pine nuts for 2-3 minutes or until spinach wilts. Remove pan from heat and stir in breadcrumbs, nutmeg and black pepper to taste. Spread spinach mixture over cut flap.

3   Roll up loin firmly and secure with string. Place in a baking dish, rub all over rind with salt and bake for 20 minutes. Reduce oven temperature to 180°C/ 350°F/Gas 4 and bake for 1 hour longer or until juices run clear when tested with a skewer in the meatiest part.

4   To make relish, place apple, pear, dates, apple juice, honey, lemon rind and cloves in a small saucepan, cover and bring to the boil. Reduce heat and simmer for 5 minutes or until apple is tender. Serve with pork.

Oven temperature
250°C, 500°F, Gas 9

When you buy pork it should be pale-fleshed with a sweet smell, not slimy or bloody. With improved technology and butchering you can now buy smaller, leaner cuts of pork – meat that is ideal for today's lifestyle.

HONEY-GLAZED HAM

Oven temperature
180°C, 350°F, Gas 4

4 kg/8 lb cooked leg ham
whole cloves

HONEY GLAZE
$^1/_2$ cup/170 g/5$^1/_2$ oz honey
1 cup/250 mL/8 fl oz orange juice
1 tablespoon Dijon mustard
2 teaspoons soy sauce
1 tablespoon brown sugar

1 Remove skin from ham. To remove skin cut a scallop pattern through the skin around the shank bone, then, starting at the broad end of the ham and using your fingers, gently ease skin away from the fat.

2 Using a sharp knife score the fat in a diamond pattern, taking care not to cut right through into the meat. Place ham in a large baking dish.

3 To make glaze, place honey, orange juice, mustard, soy sauce and brown sugar in a small saucepan and cook over a low heat, stirring, until honey and sugar melt. Brush ham with some of the glaze, then stud each diamond section with a whole clove and bake for 1 hour, brushing with remaining glaze every 20 minutes.

Serves 25

A glazed ham makes the perfect main dish for any buffet. It is delicious served hot, warm or cold. If serving hot, allow the ham to stand for 10 minutes before carving. If serving cold, glaze the ham the day before and then refrigerate. Cold meats are more succulent at room temperature, so remove the ham from the refrigerator 20 minutes before serving.

ORIENTAL SPARERIBS

Oven temperature
180°C, 350°C, Gas 4

1 kg/2 lb pork spareribs, trimmed of all visible fat and cut in 15 cm/6 in lengths

ORIENTAL MARINADE
$^1/_4$ cup/60 mL/2 fl oz hoisin sauce
$^1/_4$ cup/60 mL/2 fl oz tomato sauce
2 tablespoons soy sauce
$^1/_4$ cup/90 g/3 oz honey
2 cloves garlic, crushed
2 teaspoons grated fresh ginger
1 teaspoon chilli sauce
1 teaspoon Chinese five spice powder

1 To make marinade, place hoisin sauce, tomato sauce, soy sauce, honey, garlic, ginger, chilli sauce and five spice powder in a bowl and mix to combine. Add ribs and toss to coat. Cover and refrigerate for 8 hours or overnight.

2 Remove ribs from marinade and reserve marinade. Place ribs in a single layer on a rack set over a baking dish. Bake, basting occasionally with reserved marinade, for 40 minutes or until ribs are tender.

Serves 8

Eating and enjoying ribs can be messy. When serving ribs it is a good idea to supply bowls of water for washing fingers, and large napkins. At many rib restaurants the diner is supplied with a bib!

Honey-glazed Ham

Moroccan Stew

1 tablespoon vegetable oil
500 g/1 lb chuck steak, cut into
2.5 cm/1 in cubes
2 cups/500 mL/16 fl oz beef stock
2 teaspoons ground cinnamon
2 tablespoons honey
$^1/_2$ teaspoon ground turmeric
$^1/_2$ teaspoon ground nutmeg
60 g/2 oz raisins
60 g/2 oz dried apricots, chopped
8 baby onions
2 tablespoons orange juice
60 g/2 oz blanched almonds
freshly ground black pepper

Serves 4

For an attractive presentation, serve this stew on a bed of saffron rice. To make saffron rice, soak a few strands of saffron in 3 tablespoons warm water and add to water when cooking rice. Instead of saffron you can use $^1/_4$ teaspoon ground turmeric, in which case there is no need to soak it; simply add to water and rice.

1   Heat oil in a heavy-based saucepan and cook meat over a high heat for 4-5 minutes or until browned on all sides. Stir in stock and cinnamon, bring to the boil, then reduce heat and simmer for 10 minutes, stirring to lift any sediment from base of pan.

2   Add honey, turmeric, nutmeg, raisins and apricots to pan, cover and simmer for 30 minutes.

3   Stir in onions, orange juice and almonds and simmer, uncovered, for 30 minutes longer or until meat is tender. Season to taste with black pepper

Lamb Filo Parcels

Oven temperature
220°C, 425°F, Gas 7

8 lean lamb cutlets
2 cloves garlic, cut into slivers
2 teaspoons wholegrain mustard
90 g/3 oz blue cheese
15 g/$^1/_2$ oz butter, softened
1 teaspoon port or sherry
16 sheets filo pastry
3 tablespoons olive oil

VEGETABLE FILLING
15 g/$^1/_2$ oz butter
4 spring onions, chopped
1 red pepper, finely chopped
8 button mushrooms, finely chopped
2 large lettuce leaves, shredded

Serves 4

Reduce fat intake by cutting all visible fat from meat before cooking. The more fat you trim off before cooking, the easier it is to make healthy, low-fat meat meals.

1   Trim meat of all visible fat and insert a sliver of garlic between meat and bone of each cutlet. Cook cutlets under a preheated grill for 1-2 minutes each side or until just browned but not cooked through. Spread both sides of each cutlet with mustard. Place cheese, butter and port or sherry in a small bowl, mix to combine and top each cutlet with a spoonful of mixture.

2   To make filling, melt butter in a frying pan and cook spring onions, red pepper, mushrooms and lettuce for 2-3 minutes or until spring onions soften and lettuce wilts. Set aside to cool slightly.

3   Working with 2 sheets of pastry, brush between sheets with oil, fold in half, then in half again to form a square. Brush between folds with oil. Spread a little of the vegetable mixture over pastry, top with a cutlet, then top with more vegetable mixture. Fold pastry to enclose cutlet, leaving bone exposed, brush with oil and place on a baking tray.

4   Repeat with remaining pastry, cutlets and vegetable mixture. Bake cutlets for 10 minutes or until pastry is golden brown.

GLAZED CORNED BEEF

1.5 kg/3 lb corned (salted) silverside
2 tablespoons brown sugar
1 tablespoon cider vinegar
2 sprigs fresh mint
1 onion, peeled and studded with
4 whole cloves
6 black peppercorns
6 small carrots
6 small onions
3 parsnips, halved

REDCURRANT GLAZE
$^1/_2$ cup/155 g/5 oz redcurrant jelly
2 tablespoons orange juice
1 tablespoon sweet sherry

Moroccan Stew   ***Serves 6***

1   Place silverside in a large heavy-based saucepan. Add brown sugar, vinegar, mint, clove-studded onion, peppercorns and enough water to cover meat. Cover, bring to the boil over a medium heat, then reduce heat and simmer for $1^1/_4$-$1^1/_2$ hours.

2   Add carrots, onions and parsnips to pan and simmer for 40 minutes longer or until vegetables are tender.

3   To make glaze, place redcurrant jelly, orange juice and sherry in a small saucepan and cook over a low heat, stirring occasionally, until jelly melts and glaze is blended. Transfer meat to a warm serving platter and brush with glaze. Slice meat and serve with vegetables and any remaining glaze.

Simple and satisfying, corned beef is delicious served with creamy mashed potatoes and horseradish cream. To make horseradish cream, whip $^1/_2$ cup/125 mL/4 fl oz cream (double) until soft peaks form, then fold in 3 tablespoons horseradish relish.

BEEF IN BEER

Oven temperature
150°C, 300°F, Gas 2

Casseroles can be prepared in advance and frozen. If you are cooking food to freeze, especially spicy or hot dishes, it is a good idea to under-season them slightly, as freezing often intensifies the flavour. It is easier to add more spicy flavour on reheating than to take it away!

2 tablespoons vegetable oil
750 g/1$^1/_2$ lb lean topside beef, cut into 2.5 cm/1 in cubes
2 onions, chopped
2 carrots, cut into 1 cm/$^1/_2$ in slices
2 tablespoons flour
$^1/_2$ cup/125 mL/4 fl oz beer
2 cups/500 mL/16 fl oz beef stock
2 cloves garlic, crushed
1 tablespoon grated fresh ginger
2 tablespoons honey
1 tablespoon finely grated orange rind
freshly ground black pepper

Serves 6

1 Heat oil in a large nonstick frying pan and cook beef over a high heat until browned on all sides. Transfer beef to a large casserole dish.

2 Reduce heat to medium and cook onions and carrots for 4-5 minutes or until onions start to soften. Stir in flour and cook for 1 minute, stirring continuously, then add beer and $^1/_2$ cup/125 mL/4 fl oz stock and cook for 3-4 minutes, stirring to lift any sediment from base of pan. Stir in remaining stock, garlic, ginger, honey, orange rind and black pepper to taste.

3 Pour stock mixture over meat, cover and bake for 1$^3/_4$-2 hours or until meat is tender.

INDIVIDUAL MEAT PIES

750 g/1¹/₂ lb prepared shortcrust pastry
375 g/12 oz prepared puff pastry
1 egg, lightly beaten

BEEF FILLING
750 g/1¹/₂ lb lean beef mince
2 cups/500 mL/16 fl oz beef stock
freshly ground black pepper
2 tablespoons cornflour blended with
¹/₂ cup/125 mL/4 fl oz water
1 tablespoon Worcestershire sauce
1 teaspoon soy sauce

1   To make filling, heat a nonstick frying pan and cook meat over a medium heat, stirring constantly, for 6-8 minutes or until meat browns. Drain pan of any juices, add stock and season to taste with black pepper.

2   Bring mixture to the boil, then reduce heat, cover and simmer for 20 minutes, stirring occasionally. Stir in cornflour mixture, Worcestershire and soy sauces and cook, stirring constantly, until mixture boils and thickens. Cool.

3   Roll out shortcrust pastry to 3 mm/ ¹/₈ in thick and use to line base and sides of eight greased small metal pie dishes. Divide filling between pie dishes. Roll out puff pastry to 3 mm/¹/₈ in thick and cut rounds to fit tops of pies. Brush edges of shortcrust pastry with water, top with rounds of puff pastry and press edges together to seal. Brush tops of pies with egg and bake for 5 minutes. Reduce oven temperature to 180°C/350°F/Gas 4 and bake for 10-15 minutes longer or until tops of pies are golden and crisp.

Makes 8

Oven temperature
220°C, 425°F, Gas 7

BEEF AND MUSHROOM PIE

4 tablespoons vegetable oil
1 onion, chopped
125 g/4 oz mushrooms, sliced
500 g/1 lb lean topside steak, cut into
2 cm/³/₄ in cubes
1¹/₄ cups/315 mL/10 fl oz beef stock
freshly ground black pepper
2 tablespoons cornflour blended with
4 tablespoons water
12 sheets filo pastry
1 tablespoon poppy seeds

1   Heat 1 tablespoon oil in a large saucepan and cook onion and mushrooms for 2-3 minutes. Add meat, stock and black pepper to taste to pan, bring to the boil, then reduce heat, cover and simmer for 1¹/₂-2 hours. Remove cover, return to the boil, whisk in cornflour mixture and cook, stirring, until sauce thickens. Remove pan from heat and cool.

2   Layer pastry sheets on top of each other, brushing between layers with remaining oil. Place a 23 cm/9 in pie dish upside down on pastry and cut a circle 2 cm/³/₄ in larger than dish.

3   Line pie dish with eight of the cut pastry layers. Fill dish with meat mixture and top with remaining four pastry layers. Roll down edges of pastry and brush top with a little oil. Sprinkle with poppy seeds and bake for 30 minutes.

Serves 6

Oven temperature
180°C, 350°F, Gas 4

Especially for weight watchers, this pie is made with filo pastry and lean beef to cut calories and fat. At 1131 kilojoules/214 calories per serve it is a healthy and satisfying pie that can be enjoyed by all.

STEAK AND KIDNEY PIE

Oven temperature
220°C, 425°F, Gas 7

Did you know early pies were
called pastry coffins? The
word 'coffin' originally meant
any box, basket or case.

1 kg/2 lb lean topside steak, cut into
2.5 cm/1 in cubes
6 lamb's kidneys or 1 ox kidney,
cored and roughly chopped
4 tablespoons flour
1 tablespoon vegetable oil
2 cloves garlic, crushed
2 onions, chopped
$^1/_2$ teaspoon dry mustard
2 tablespoons chopped fresh parsley
2 tablespoons Worcestershire sauce
$1^1/_2$ cups/375 mL/12 fl oz beef stock
2 teaspoons tomato paste (purée)
375 g/12 oz prepared puff pastry
2 tablespoons milk

1   Place steak, kidneys and flour in a
plastic food bag and shake to coat meat
with flour. Shake off excess flour and set
aside. Heat oil in a large frying pan and
cook meat over a high heat, stirring, until
brown on all sides. Reduce heat to
medium, add garlic and onions and cook
for 3 minutes longer. Stir in mustard,
parsley, Worcestershire sauce, stock and
tomato paste (purée), bring to simmering,
cover and simmer, stirring occasionally,
for $2^1/2$ hours or until meat is tender.
Remove pan from heat and set aside to
cool completely.

2   Place cooled filling in a 4 cup/1 litre/
$1^3/_4$ pt capacity pie dish. On a lightly
floured surface, roll out pastry to
5 cm/2 in larger than pie dish. Cut off a
1 cm/$^1/_2$ in strip from pastry edge. Brush
rim of dish with water and press pastry
strip onto rim. Brush pastry strip with
water. Lift pastry top over filling and press
gently to seal edges. Trim and knock back
edges to make a decorative edge. Brush
with milk and bake for 30 minutes or
until pastry is golden and crisp.

Serves 6

Steak and Kidney Pie

Pork and Chicken Loaf

PORK AND CHICKEN LOAF

30 g/1 oz butter
1 onion, chopped
1 clove garlic, crushed
750 g/1¹/₂ lb pork fillets, minced
3 tablespoons chopped fresh parsley
2 eggs
2 teaspoons canned (bottled)
green peppercorns, drained
1 tablespoon dry vermouth
500 g/1 lb prepared puff pastry
2 boneless chicken breast fillets
1 egg white, lightly beaten

Serves 6

1 Melt butter in a frying pan and cook onion and garlic over a medium heat for 4-5 minutes or until onion softens. Place pork, parsley, eggs, peppercorns, vermouth and onion mixture in a bowl and mix to combine.

2 Roll out pastry to form a rectangle 30 x 40 cm/12 x 16 in. Cut a 7.5 cm/3 in square from each corner – this eliminates bulkiness when folded. Press pork mixture down centre of pastry to form a rectangular shape. Top with chicken fillets and wrap up like a parcel. Cut pastry leaves from pastry scraps and use to decorate top of loaf.

3 Brush with egg white and place on a greased roasting rack set over a baking dish and bake for 1-1¹/₂ hours or until pastry is crisp and golden.

Oven temperature
180°C, 350°F, Gas 4

Served hot with mashed potatoes and a green vegetable, this loaf makes a hearty winter meal. Served cold with a selection of chutneys and a tossed lettuce salad, it is wonderful for a summer dinner or picnic.

LAMB AND SPINACH STRUDEL

Oven temperature
180°C, 350°F, Gas 4

When making pies and pastries it is important to allow the filling to cool completely before wrapping in, or topping with, pastry. A hot filling causes the fat in the pastry to run and the pastry tends to go soggy. Recipes often recommend refrigerating the whole dish for 15-30 minutes after assembly. This ensures that the pastry holds its shape during cooking and that it is not soggy or greasy.

3 tablespoons vegetable oil
1 onion, finely chopped
375 g/12 oz lean boneless lamb,
finely chopped
185 g/6 oz mushrooms, finely chopped
2 tablespoons German mustard
200 g/6^1/$_2$ oz frozen spinach, excess
liquid squeezed out, and chopped
1 red pepper, finely chopped
2 tablespoons chopped fresh parsley
^{1}/$_2$ cup/30 g/1 oz bread crumbs, made
from stale bread
6 sheets filo pastry
1 tablespoon sesame seeds

Serves 4

1   Heat 2 tablespoons oil in a large frying pan and cook onion and lamb over a high heat for 4-5 minutes or until lamb is browned. Add mushrooms and cook for 2 minutes longer. Transfer lamb mixture to a large bowl and stir in mustard, spinach, red pepper, parsley and bread crumbs.

2   Fold filo sheets in half, brush each sheet with remaining oil and layer sheets one on top of the other. Spoon filling along the short side of pastry, leaving a 3 cm/1^1/$_4$ in border of pastry. Shape filling into a sausage, tuck in long sides of pastry and roll up.

3   Place strudel, seam side down, on a lightly greased baking tray, brush with oil and sprinkle with sesame seeds. Bake for 40 minutes or until pastry is golden.

CURRIED PORK PIES

1 tablespoon vegetable oil
1 onion, chopped
1 clove garlic, crushed
250 g/8 oz lean pork mince
2 teaspoons curry powder
1 tablespoon flour
1 small apple, peeled, cored and chopped
60 g/2 oz sultanas
$^1/_2$ cup/125 mL/4 fl oz water
375 g/12 oz prepared shortcrust pastry
2 tablespoons milk

1   Heat oil in a large frying pan and cook onion and garlic for 4-5 minutes or until onion softens. Add pork and cook for 5 minutes longer or until browned. Stir in curry powder and flour and cook for 1 minute longer.

Makes 10

2   Add apple, sultanas and water to pan, cover and simmer for 10 minutes or until pork is cooked and mixture thickens. Remove pan from heat and set aside to cool.

3   Roll out pastry to 3 mm/$^1/_8$ in thick and cut out twelve pastry rounds using a 10 cm/4 in pastry cutter and twelve tops using a 7.5 cm/3 in pastry cutter. Press the larger pastry rounds into lightly greased flat-based patty tins (tartlet tins) and fill with pork mixture. Brush pastry edges with a little milk and top with smaller rounds. Press pastry edges together to seal. Using a sharp-pointed knife make a small cut in the top of each pie. Brush tops of pies with milk and bake for 15 minutes or until golden. Stand for 5 minutes before removing from tins and serving.

Oven temperature
200°C, 400°F, Gas 6

When glazing puff pastry with egg or milk take care that you only brush the top of the pastry and that none of the glaze runs down the side. Any glaze that runs down the side of the pastry or the sides of pastry decorations will prevent the pastry from rising evenly.

BARBECUES

*Barbecuing is a great way to cook for family and
friends and with a little preplanning it is one of the easiest
ways to entertain. No matter whether you choose Marinated
Fillet of Beef, Pork and Orange Kebabs, or one of the
other delicious recipes in this chapter, it is sure
to be a success at your next barbecue.*

Coconut Lamb Kebabs

Coconut Lamb Kebabs

500 g/1 lb lean lamb mince
1 tablespoon tomato paste (purée)
3 tablespoons desiccated coconut
1 teaspoon ground cumin
2 tablespoons chopped fresh coriander
1 tablespoon chopped fresh parsley
3 tablespoons lime or lemon juice
freshly ground pepper

1   Preheat barbecue to a medium heat.

2   Place lamb, tomato paste (purée), coconut, cumin, coriander, parsley, lime or lemon juice and black pepper to taste in a large bowl and mix well to combine. Roll tablespoons of mixture into balls and push three balls onto a lightly oiled bamboo skewer. Repeat with remaining mixture.

3   Cook on lightly oiled barbecue grill for 4-5 minutes each side or until cooked to your liking.

Serves 4

These meatballs on a stick are always popular with children. Serve with bowls of tomato and chilli sauces for dipping, or a selection of chutneys.

Pork and Orange Kebabs

500 g/1 lb pork fillet, cut into
2.5 cm/1 in cubes
2 oranges, rind and pith removed, cut into 2.5 cm/1 in cubes
1 red pepper, cut into 2.5 cm/1 in cubes

ORANGE MARINADE
^{1}/4 cup/60 mL/2 fl oz orange juice
2 tablespoons lemon juice
2 cloves garlic, crushed
3 tablespoons tomato purée
1 onion, grated
1 tablespoon olive oil
2 tablespoons honey

1   To make marinade, place orange juice, lemon juice, garlic, tomato purée, onion, oil and honey in a bowl and mix to combine.

2   Add pork, toss to coat and set aside to marinate for 1 hour.

3   Preheat barbecue to a medium heat.

4   Thread pork, orange and red pepper cubes, alternately, onto lightly oiled bamboo skewers and cook on lightly oiled barbecue grill, basting frequently with marinade for 5-6 minutes each side or until pork is cooked.

Serves 4

When using bamboo skewers, soak them in cold water for at least an hour before using them under a grill or on a barbecue; this will prevent them from burning. Lightly oiling the skewers ensures that the food does not stick to them during cooking.

Marinated T-bones

6 T-bone steaks, each 2.5 cm/1 in thick

ORIENTAL MARINADE
3 tablespoons Thai fish sauce
2 tablespoons lemon juice
4 cloves garlic, crushed
2 teaspoons sesame oil
1 teaspoon chilli paste (sambal oelek)

A marinade tenderises the tough, moistens the dry and flavours the bland. It can be that secret barbecue ingredient that turns an otherwise ordinary piece of meat into a taste sensation. A marinade consists of three main ingredients: an acid, such as lemon juice, wine or vinegar, to tenderise; an oil to moisturise; and flavourings to give character.

1   To make marinade, place fish sauce, lemon juice, garlic, oil and chilli paste (sambal oelek) in a bowl and mix to combine. Place T-bone steaks in a single layer in a shallow glass or ceramic dish and pour over marinade. Cover and refrigerate for 2 hours.

2   Preheat barbecue to a medium heat.

3   Drain steaks and cook on lightly oiled barbecue grill, brushing frequently with marinade for 3-5 minutes each side or until cooked to your liking.

Serves 6

Spicy Yogurt Lamb

2 kg/4 lb leg lamb, butterflied
2 tablespoons sesame seeds

SPICY YOGURT MARINADE
500 g/1 lb natural yogurt
1 tablespoon lemon juice
1 tablespoon grated fresh ginger
2 tablespoons chopped fresh coriander
2 teaspoons ground cinnamon
1 teaspoon ground cardamom
$^1/_2$ teaspoon ground cloves
2 tablespoons pine nuts
freshly ground black pepper

CORIANDER YOGURT SAUCE
500 g/1 lb natural yogurt
1 teaspoon finely grated lemon rind
2 tablespoons chopped fresh coriander

Your butcher will butterfly a leg of lamb for you in minutes. When purchasing 'special cuts', ring your butcher and order in advance. In most cases if you give the butcher one to two days warning he will be able to supply you with any special cuts you may require.

1   To make marinade, place yogurt, lemon juice, ginger, coriander, cinnamon, cardamom, cloves, pine nuts and black pepper to taste in a food processor or blender and process until smooth.

2   Lay lamb out flat, place in a shallow glass or ceramic dish and coat with marinade. Cover and refrigerate for 24 hours.

3   Stand lamb at room temperature for 2 hours. Remove lamb from marinade and reserve marinade. Using bamboo skewers, skewer lamb in several places so that it holds its shape during cooking.

4   Preheat barbecue to a medium heat. Cook lamb on lightly oiled barbecue grill, turning several times and basting with reserved marinade for 25 minutes. Sprinkle lamb with sesame seeds and cook for 5-10 minutes longer or until lamb is cooked to your liking. Allow lamb to stand for 10 minutes before carving.

5   To make sauce, place yogurt, lemon rind, coriander and black pepper to taste in a bowl and mix to combine. Serve with lamb.

Serves 8

Marinated Fillet of Beef

750 g/1¹/2 lb beef fillet

RED WINE MARINADE
1¹/2 cups/375 mL/12 fl oz red wine
¹/2 cup/125 mL/4 fl oz olive oil
1 small onion, diced
1 bay leaf, torn into pieces
1 teaspoon black peppercorns, cracked
1 clove garlic, crushed
3 teaspoons finely chopped fresh thyme
or 1 teaspoon dried thyme

1   To make marinade, place wine, oil, onion, bay leaf, peppercorns, garlic and thyme in a small bowl and mix to combine.

2   Place beef in a shallow glass or ceramic dish, pour over marinade, cover and marinate in refrigerator overnight. Turn occasionally during marinating.

3   Preheat barbecue to a high heat. Drain beef and sear on all sides, on lightly oiled barbecue grill or plate (griddle). Move beef to a cooler section of the barbecue and cook, turning frequently, for 15-20 minutes or until cooked to your liking. Place beef on side of barbecue to keep warm for 10 minutes before carving.

*Marinated T-bones,
Spicy Yogurt Lamb*

Serves 10

Always drain marinated food well before cooking, especially when cooking on a barbecue plate (griddle) or in a frying pan. Wet food will stew rather than brown. The remaining marinade can be brushed over the food several times during cooking.

LAMB WITH SATAY SAUCE

750 g/1¹/₂ lb lean lamb mince
3 tablespoons chopped fresh parsley
1 teaspoon dried oregano
2 teaspoons ground cumin
2 tablespoons tomato paste (purée)
2 onions, grated
³/₄ cup/90 g/3 oz dried bread crumbs
2 egg whites, lightly beaten

SATAY SAUCE
1 tablespoon peanut (groundnut) oil
2 cloves garlic, crushed
1 onion, finely chopped
4 tablespoons crunchy peanut butter
1 teaspoon tomato paste (purée)
2 tablespoons sweet fruit chutney
2 tablespoons dry sherry
1 tablespoon lemon juice
4 tablespoons coconut milk
2 teaspoons ground coriander
1 teaspoon chilli paste (sambal oelek)

Makes 8 kebabs

1 Preheat barbecue to a medium heat.

2 Place lamb, parsley, oregano, cumin, tomato paste (purée), onions, bread crumbs and egg whites in a large bowl and mix to combine. Divide mixture into eight portions and shape each portion into a sausage shape. Thread each sausage onto a lightly oiled bamboo skewer.

3 Cook lamb kebabs on lightly oiled barbecue grill or plate (griddle), turning frequently, for 10 minutes or until cooked through.

4 To make sauce, heat oil in a saucepan and cook garlic and onion over a medium heat for 1 minute. Stir in peanut butter, tomato paste (purée), chutney, sherry, lemon juice, coconut milk, coriander and chilli paste (sambal oelek) and cook, stirring constantly, over a low heat for 10 minutes or until sauce thickens slightly. Serve with kebabs.

As with any type of cooking, basic safety rules should always be observed when barbecuing. Remember always to check the barbecue area before lighting the barbecue. Do not have the barbecue too close to the house and sweep up any dry leaves or anything that might catch fire if hit by a spark. Always check the manufacturer's safety instructions that come with your barbecue.

VEAL AND APRICOT SKEWERS

375 g/12 oz topside veal, cut into
2 cm/³/₄ in cubes
125 g/4 oz dried apricots

CHILLI YOGURT MARINADE
1¹/₂ cups/300 g/9¹/₂ oz natural yogurt
1 onion, grated
2 cloves garlic, crushed
2 teaspoons chilli paste (sambal oelek)
1 tablespoon lime juice
1 teaspoon ground cumin
1 tablespoon chopped fresh coriander

Serves 4

1 To make marinade, place yogurt, onion, garlic, chilli paste (sambal oelek), lime juice, cumin and coriander in a food processor or blender and process to combine. Transfer to large bowl, add veal and apricots and toss to combine. Cover and marinate for 2 hours.

2 Preheat barbecue to a medium heat. Drain veal and apricots and reserve marinade. Thread veal and apricots, alternately, onto lightly oiled bamboo skewers and cook on lightly oiled barbecue grill, turning and basting with reserved marinade, for 10 minutes or until cooked.

As marinades contain acid ingredients, the food and marinade should be placed in stainless steel, enamel, glass or ceramic dishes. The marinade should come up around the sides of the food, but need not completely cover it. Turn the food several times during marinating.

Lamb with Satay Sauce,
Veal and Apricot Skewers

QUICK MEALS

*Meat, whether it's lamb, pork or beef, is the
perfect basis for quick, nutritious meals. For quick
cooking, you should choose the more tender cuts and mince.
In this chapter you will find a selection of dishes that
take next to no time to prepare and cook.*

Chilli Con Carne

48

CHILLI CON CARNE

2 tablespoons vegetable oil
2 onions, chopped
2 cloves garlic, crushed
$^1/_4$ teaspoon chilli powder
500 g/1 lb lean beef mince
3 tablespoons tomato paste (purée)
$^1/_4$ cup/60 mL/2 fl oz red wine
440 g/14 oz canned tomatoes, undrained
and mashed
315 g/10 oz canned red kidney beans,
drained and rinsed
freshly ground black pepper
125 g/4 oz tasty cheese (mature
Cheddar), grated
$^1/_2$ cup/125 g/4 oz sour cream

1   Heat oil in a large frying pan and cook onions, garlic and chilli powder over a medium heat for 2 minutes.

2   Add mince and cook for 5 minutes longer. Stir in tomato paste (purée), wine, tomatoes and beans, bring to simmering and simmer for 10 minutes. Season to taste with black pepper. Serve topped with grated cheese and sour cream.

Serves 4

An all-time favourite, you can make Chilli Con Carne as hot or as mild as you like, simply by adjusting the amount of chilli powder that you use. For a complete meal, serve with a green salad of mixed lettuce and fresh herbs.

BEEF PATTIES WITH GOAT'S CHEESE

500 g/1 lb lean beef mince
1 egg, lightly beaten
3 tablespoons bread crumbs, made
from stale bread
freshly ground black pepper
1 tomato, cut into four thick slices
100 g/3$^1/_2$ oz goat's cheese, sliced
1 tablespoon snipped fresh chives

1   Place mince, egg, bread crumbs and black pepper to taste in a bowl and mix to combine. Divide mixture into four portions and shape into patties about 1 cm/$^1/_2$ in thick. Place patties on a plate lined with plastic food wrap, cover and refrigerate for 15 minutes.

2   Cook patties under a preheated grill for 3-4 minutes each side or until cooked to your liking. Top each pattie with a tomato slice and a cheese slice and cook under grill for 2-3 minutes longer or until cheese melts. Sprinkle with chives and serve immediately.

Serves 4

These patties are also delicious served on toasted wholemeal rolls with lettuce and chutney.

CHILLI BURGERS

500 g/1 lb lean beef mince
1 onion, finely chopped
freshly ground black pepper
2 tablespoons vegetable oil
4 sesame seed rolls, split and toasted
4 large lettuce leaves, shredded
4 slices Gruyère cheese
1 onion, thinly sliced into rings

CHILLI SAUCE
2 tablespoons olive oil
1 onion, finely chopped
2 cloves garlic, crushed
440 g/14 oz canned tomatoes, undrained
and mashed
1 teaspoon chilli paste (sambal oelek)
1 tablespoon chilli relish
$^{1}/_{2}$ teaspoon cumin seeds

1   To make sauce, heat oil in a saucepan
and cook onion and garlic over a medium
heat for 5 minutes. Stir in tomatoes,
chilli paste (sambal oelek), chilli relish
and cumin seeds, bring to simmering and
simmer, stirring occasionally, for 10
minutes or until sauce thickens and
reduces.

2   Place mince, chopped onion and
black pepper to taste in a bowl and mix to
combine. Divide meat mixture into four
portions and shape each into a 10 cm/4 in
round pattie. Heat oil in a large frying
pan and cook patties over a medium heat
for 4-5 minutes each side or until cooked
to your liking.

3   To assemble burgers, top bottom half
of each roll with lettuce, a meat pattie, a
slice of cheese, some sauce, a few onion
rings and, finally, top half of roll. Serve
immediately.

Homemade burgers make a
nutritious meal when teamed
with a tossed green salad.

Serves 4

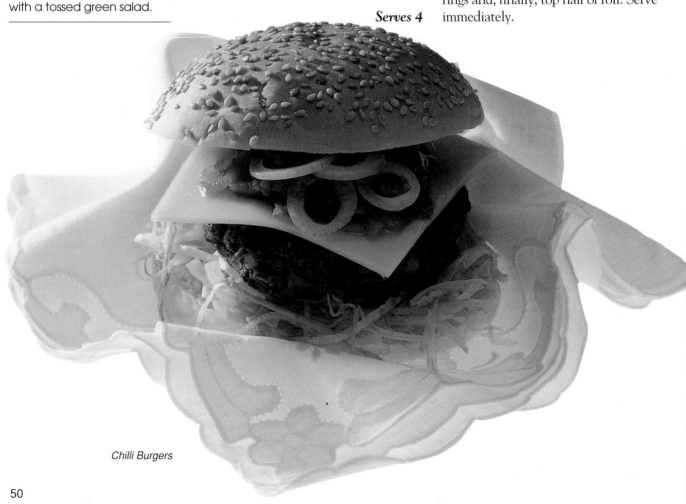

Chilli Burgers

ORIENTAL PORK

1 tablespoon vegetable oil
750 g/1¹/₂ lb pork fillets, cut into
1 cm/¹/₂ in slices
1 red pepper, cut into
2 cm/³/₄ in squares
3 cloves garlic, peeled
12 baby onions
1 teaspoon grated fresh ginger
1 teaspoon chilli paste (sambal oelek)
350 g/11 oz pineapple pieces, drained
and juice reserved
1 cup/250 mL/8 fl oz chicken stock
2 tablespoons soy sauce
220 g/7 oz green beans, trimmed

Serves 6

1   Heat oil in a large frying pan and cook pork over medium-high heat for 4-5 minutes or until browned on all sides. Remove, set aside and keep warm.

2   Add red pepper, garlic, onions, ginger and chilli paste (sambal oelek) to pan and stir-fry for 5-6 minutes. Stir in reserved pineapple juice, chicken stock, soy sauce and beans, bring to simmering and simmer for 10 minutes or until beans are tender.

3   Stir in pineapple pieces, return pork to pan and cook for 5 minutes longer or until heated through.

Stock cubes are high in salt and, although convenient, are best avoided. If possible use homemade stock or choose prepared low-salt stock or low-salt stock cubes. Homemade tastes better, is easy to make and can be made ahead of time and then frozen.

LAMB AND SPINACH PIZZA

Oven temperature
180°C, 350°F, Gas 4

1 cup/185 g/6 oz cracked (bulgur) wheat
2 cups/500 mL/16 fl oz hot water
2 teaspoons olive oil
1 onion, chopped
1 clove garlic, crushed
500 g/1 lb lean lamb mince
$^1/_2$ teaspoon dried mixed herbs
1 tablespoon lemon juice
1 tablespoon chopped fresh mint
$^1/_2$ teaspoon chilli powder

HUMMUS TOPPING
$^3/_4$ cup/220 g/7 oz hummus
2 tomatoes, sliced
8 spinach leaves, blanched and chopped
3 tablespoons pine nuts
4 tablespoons grated tasty cheese
(mature Cheddar)

1   Place cracked wheat and water in a bowl and set aside to soak for 10-15 minutes.

2   Heat oil in a nonstick frying pan and cook onion and garlic over a medium heat for 3-4 minutes or until onion is soft. Drain cracked wheat and stir in onion mixture, mince, mixed herbs, lemon juice, mint and chilli powder. Mix well to combine.

3   Press meat mixture into a 30 cm/12 in pizza tray and cook for 20 minutes or until base is firm. Drain off any juices.

4   To make topping, spread meat pizza base with hummus then top with tomato slices and spinach. Sprinkle with pine nuts and cheese and cook under a preheated grill for 3-4 minutes or until cheese melts.

For a complete meal serve pizza cut into wedges accompanied by crusty bread and a tossed green salad.

Serves 6

Left: Lamb and Spinach Pizza
Below: Veal and Cheese Rolls

VEAL AND CHEESE ROLLS

75 g/2$^1/_2$ oz mozzarella cheese, grated
2 rashers bacon, finely chopped
2 tablespoons chopped fresh parsley
2 tablespoons grated Parmesan cheese
4 veal schnitzels (escalopes), pounded
$^1/_2$ cup/60 g/2 oz flour
4 tablespoons olive oil
$^3/_4$ cup/185 mL/6 fl oz dry white wine

1   Place mozzarella cheese, bacon, parsley and Parmesan cheese in a bowl and mix to combine.

2   Lay veal schnitzels (escalopes) out flat and top with cheese mixture, leaving a border around the edge of each schnitzel (escalope). Roll up each schnitzel (escalope), tucking in sides, secure with string and roll in flour.

3   Heat oil in large frying pan and cook veal rolls over a medium heat, turning frequently, for 6-7 minutes or until browned on all sides. Stir in wine and cook for 5 minutes longer. Remove veal rolls from pan, strain juices and serve spooned over rolls.

Serves 4

The more cutting and preparation meat has had, the shorter the storage time; for example, mince has a shorter storage time than chops or steak.

DEVILLED BACON SKEWERS

8 rashers bacon, rind removed
16 button mushrooms
16 cherry tomatoes
4 tablespoons fruit chutney
2 teaspoons curry powder

Perfect for a special breakfast or brunch or just as a light meal, these kebabs take only minutes to prepare. Depending on what time of day you serve them, they are delicious with toasted English muffins, crusty French bread or a fresh tomato salad.

1   Thread bacon, mushrooms and tomatoes onto lightly oiled bamboo skewers. Thread bacon in a weaving fashion, inserting mushrooms and tomatoes, alternately, as you go.

2   Place chutney and curry powder in a small saucepan and cook over a low heat for 4-5 minutes. Brush kebabs with chutney mixture and cook under a preheated grill for 4-5 minutes or until bacon is cooked.

Makes 8 kebabs

BACON OMELETTE

2 eggs
2 teaspoons water
freshly ground black pepper
15 g/¹/2 oz butter

BACON FILLING
1 rasher bacon, chopped
2 tablespoons grated Gruyère cheese

An omelette is the perfect meal for people on the run. Served with a wholemeal roll and a piece of fruit for dessert, it is a quick and nutritious meal.

1   To make filling, cook bacon in a small frying pan over a medium heat for 3-4 minutes or until crisp. Drain, place in a small bowl, add cheese and black pepper to taste. Mix to combine and set aside.

2   Place eggs, water and black pepper to taste in a small bowl and whisk to combine.

3   Heat an omelette pan over a medium heat until hot. Add butter, tipping the pan so the base is completely coated. Heat until the butter is foaming, but not browned, then add the egg mixture. As it sets use a palette knife or fork to gently draw up the edge of the omelette until no liquid remains and the omelette is lightly set.

4   Top omelette with filling, fold and slip onto serving plate. Serve immediately.

Serves 1

Devilled Bacon Skewers,
Bacon Omelette

Bacon and Egg Rolls

15 g/¹/₂ oz butter
4 rashers bacon, chopped
1 large potato, cooked and diced
6 eggs
freshly ground black pepper
4 long bread rolls, split
4 lettuce leaves

1 Melt butter in a frying pan over a low heat and cook bacon for 4-5 minutes. Add potato and cook over a medium heat, stirring gently, for 4-5 minutes longer or until potato cubes are golden.

2 Place eggs and black pepper to taste in a bowl and whisk to combine. Pour egg mixture over potato mixture in pan, reduce heat to low and cook for 10 minutes or until omelette is almost set. Place frying pan under a preheated medium grill and cook omelette for 2-3 minutes or until top is set.

3 Turn out omelette and cut into slices. Fill rolls with lettuce and omelette slices.

Serves 4

These rolls are delicious either hot or cold. If serving cold, allow the omelette to cool before assembling the rolls.

Bacon and Egg Roll

Beef Stroganoff

BEEF STROGANOFF

1 tablespoon vegetable oil
750 g/1¹/₂ lb scotch fillet, cut into strips
2 onions, thinly sliced
2 cloves garlic, crushed
1 cup/250 mL/8 fl oz beef stock
2 tablespoons tomato paste (purée)
1 tablespoon cornflour blended with
¹/₄ cup/60 mL/2 fl oz water
250 g/8 oz mushrooms, sliced
freshly ground black pepper
¹/₄ cup/125 g/4 oz sour cream

Serves 6

1 Heat oil in a large frying pan and cook beef in batches over a high heat for 3-4 minutes. Remove, set aside and keep warm.

2 Add onions and garlic to pan and cook over a medium heat for 5 minutes or until onions are soft. Stir in stock, tomato paste (purée) and cornflour mixture and cook, stirring constantly, for 3-4 minutes or until sauce thickens. Add mushrooms and black pepper to taste and cook for 5 minutes longer. Remove pan from heat and stir in sour cream. Return beef to pan and toss to coat with sauce.

Try low-fat natural yogurt instead of sour cream in recipes such as this one. Stir it through at the end of cooking and do not allow to boil or the yogurt becomes grainy.

CONDIMENTS

Pork and Apple Sauce, beef and Horseradish
sauce, and ham and Cumberland Sauce are all traditional
combinations. In this chapter you will find recipes for these
sauces plus other delicious accompaniments
to serve with meat.

Honey Apple Sauce

Cumberland Sauce

Spicy Cranberry
Sauce

Cherry Chutney

Béarnaise Sauce

Fresh Horseradish
Sauce

*Clockwise from top: Spicy
Cranberry Sauce, Honey Apple
Sauce, Cherry Chutney,
Cumberland Sauce*

Honey Apple Sauce

3 Granny Smith apples, cored, peeled
and chopped
2 tablespoons water
2 tablespoons honey
15 g/^{1}/$_2$ oz butter
1 teaspoon finely grated lemon rind
pinch ground cloves

1   Place apples and water in a small saucepan, bring to the boil over a medium heat, reduce heat, cover and simmer for 15-20 minutes or until apples are very soft.

2   Remove pan from heat and beat in honey, butter, lemon rind and cloves. Spoon into hot sterilised jars, cover and store in the refrigerator for 1 week.

Makes 2 cups/500 mL/16 fl oz

A variation on the traditional apple sauce recipe, this is delicious with pork and is an interesting accompaniment to serve with roast duck.

Cumberland Sauce

4 tablespoons redcurrant jelly
1 tablespoon marmalade
3 tablespoons orange juice
1 tablespoon lemon juice
4 tablespoons port

1   Place jelly in a small saucepan and cook over a low heat until melted. Stir in marmalade, orange juice, lemon juice and port, bring to simmering and simmer for 1 minute.

2   Remove pan from heat and set aside to cool. Store in an airtight container in the refrigerator for 1 week.

Makes ^{1}/$_2$ cup/125 mL/4 fl oz

Cumberland Sauce is a traditional accompaniment for pork and ham.

Spicy Cranberry Sauce

1 cup/250 mL/8 fl oz cranberry sauce
1 teaspoon finely chopped fresh ginger
1 teaspoon ground cardamom
^{1}/$_2$ teaspoon ground cinnamon
2 teaspoons Worcestershire sauce

1   Place cranberry sauce, ginger, cardamom, cinnamon and Worcestershire sauce in a small saucepan and bring to the boil over a medium heat. Reduce heat and simmer for 1 minute.

2   Pour into hot sterilised jars, cover and store in refrigerator for 2 weeks.

Makes 1 cup/250 mL/8 fl oz

This cranberry sauce is delicious with ham, lamb and all kinds of poultry.

CHERRY CHUTNEY

2 x 440 g/14 oz canned pitted dark cherries
1 cup/250 mL/8 fl oz white vinegar
1 onion, finely chopped
³/4 cup/185 g/6 oz sugar
155 g/5 oz sultanas
1 tablespoon white mustard seeds
3 teaspoons ground cinnamon
3 teaspoons ground allspice
1 teaspoon whole cloves
1 teaspoon salt

Easy to make, Cherry Chutney is a must on your Christmas table. It is a tasty condiment to serve with ham, pork, duck or turkey.

Drain cherries and pour juice from one can into a saucepan. Reserve juice from other can for another use. Add cherries, vinegar, onion, sugar, sultanas, mustard seeds, cinnamon, allspice, cloves and salt to pan, cover and bring to simmering over a low heat. Simmer, stirring occasionally, for 1 hour. Remove cover and cook, stirring occasionally, for 45 minutes longer or until chutney is thick. Pour into hot sterilised jars, cover and store in refrigerator for 1 month.

Makes 2¹/2 cups/850 g/30 oz

BEARNAISE SAUCE

1 spring onion, chopped
2 teaspoons finely chopped fresh tarragon or 1 teaspoon dried tarragon
2 tablespoons white wine vinegar
2 tablespoons dry white wine
freshly ground black pepper
3 egg yolks, lightly beaten
185 g/6 oz butter, cut into pieces
pinch cayenne pepper
1 tablespoon finely chopped fresh parsley (optional)

One of the traditional sauces to serve with roast beef and grilled or pan-cooked steak, Béarnaise Sauce is also good with chicken and fish.

1   Place spring onion, tarragon, vinegar, wine and black pepper to taste in a small saucepan and cook over a medium heat until liquid is reduced by half. Strain and discard solids.

2   Place egg yolks in a bowl set over a saucepan of simmering water. Whisk in vinegar mixture and cook, whisking constantly until blended.

3   Add butter piece by piece, whisking constantly and making sure that each piece of butter is melted and blended in before adding the next. Season to taste with cayenne pepper and stir in parsley, if using. Serve immediately.

Makes 2 cups/500 mL/16 fl oz

FRESH HORSERADISH SAUCE

3 tablespoons grated fresh horseradish
2 tablespoons caster sugar
$^1/_2$ teaspoon dry mustard
$^1/_2$ cup/60 g/2 oz breadcrumbs, made
from stale bread
2 tablespoons milk
$^3/_4$ cup/185 mL/6 fl oz cream (double),
lightly whipped
1 tablespoon red wine vinegar

Place horseradish, sugar and mustard in a bowl, mix to combine and set aside. Place breadcrumbs in a separate bowl and pour over milk, mix well then squeeze milk from bread crumbs. Stir breadcrumbs into horseradish mixture, fold in cream and vinegar. Store in an airtight container in the refrigerator for 2 days.

Makes 1 cup/250 mL/8 fl oz

Horseradish Sauce is the all-time favourite sauce to serve with hot or cold roast beef. It is also delicious in smoked salmon sandwiches.

Fresh Horseradish Sauce

BEEF FILLET WRAPPED IN PASTRY

Oven temperature
220°C, 425°F, Gas 7

Succulent beef surrounded by mushrooms and wrapped in puff pastry, is a dish that is sure to impress. With these step-by-step instructions you can see just how easy it is to make.

60 g/2 oz butter
1 kg/2 lb fillet steak, in one piece, trimmed of all visible fat
1 onion, chopped
375 g/12 oz button mushrooms, finely chopped
freshly ground black pepper
pinch ground nutmeg
1 tablespoon chopped fresh parsley
500 g/1 lb prepared puff pastry
1 egg, lightly beaten

RED WINE SAUCE
1 cup/250 mL/8 fl oz red wine
1 teaspoon finely chopped fresh thyme
or $^1/4$ teaspoon dried thyme
1 teaspoon finely chopped fresh parsley
100 g/3$^1/2$ oz butter, cut into
2 teaspoons cornflour blended with
1 tablespoon water

minutes or until mushrooms give up all their juices and these have evaporated. Season to taste with black pepper and nutmeg, stir in parsley and set aside to cool completely.

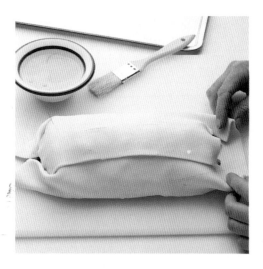

Roll pastry on a lightly floured surface in quick, straight movements away from you. To turn the pastry, hang it over your rolling pin and give a quarter turn, then roll as described above. Continue in this way until the pastry is the required thickness. Rolling pastry in this way will give you a rough rectangle from which you can cut the required shapes. Never roll in a sideways action as this tends to toughen the pastry.

1   Melt half the butter in a large frying pan. When sizzling, add fillet and cook over a medium heat for 10 minutes, turning to brown and seal all sides. Remove meat from pan and set aside to cool completely.

2   Melt remaining butter in frying pan and cook onion for 5 minutes or until soft. Add mushrooms and cook, stirring, for 15

3   Roll out pastry to a length 10 cm/4 in longer than meat and wide enough to wrap around fillet. Spread half the mushroom mixture down centre of pastry and place fillet on top. Spread remaining mushroom mixture on top of fillet. Cut out corners of pastry. Brush pastry edges

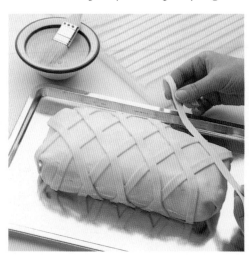

with egg. Wrap pastry around fillet like a parcel, tucking in ends. Place pastry-wrapped fillet seam side down on a lightly greased baking sheet and freeze for 10 minutes.

4 Roll out remaining pastry to 10 x 30 cm/ 4 x 12 in length and cut into strips 1 cm/ $^1/_2$ in wide. Remove fillet from freezer and brush pastry all over with egg. Arrange 5 pastry strips diagonally over pastry parcel, then arrange remaining strips diagonally in opposite direction. Brush top of strips only with egg and bake for 30 minutes for medium-rare beef. Place on a warmed serving platter and set aside to rest in a warm place for 10 minutes.

5 To make sauce, place wine in a small saucepan and cook over a medium heat until reduced by half. Add thyme, parsley and black pepper to taste. Remove pan from heat and quickly whisk in one piece of butter at a time, ensuring that each piece is completely whisked in and melted before adding the next. Whisk in cornflour mixture and cook over a medium heat, stirring until sauce thickens. Serve with sliced beef.

Serves 6

Beef Fillet wrapped in Pastry

SPRING ROLLS

Wonton or spring roll
wrappers are available from
Asian food stores and some
supermarkets.

250 g/8 oz pork fillet
1 tablespoon vegetable oil
1 red pepper, cut into strips
4 spring onions, chopped
100 g/3^1/$_2$ oz bean sprouts
6 lettuce leaves, shredded
2 teaspoons cornflour blended with
1 tablespoon water
1 tablespoon soy sauce
20 wonton or spring roll wrappers
oil for deep-frying

1 Slice pork thinly and cut crosswise
into narrow strips.

2 Heat vegetable oil in a frying pan and
stir-fry pork for 2-3 minutes or until it
changes colour. Remove pork from pan
and set aside.

3 Add red pepper and spring onions to
pan and stir-fry for 3 minutes. Stir in bean
sprouts, lettuce and cornflour mixture,
bring to the boil and cook, stirring, until
mixture thickens. Stir in soy sauce and
remove pan from heat. Return pork to
pan and set aside to cool completely.

4 Place 2 tablespoons filling in the
centre of each wonton wrapper, fold one
corner over the filling, then tuck in the
sides and roll up, sealing with water.

5 Heat oil in a large saucepan until a
cube of bread browns in 50 seconds and
cook a few Spring Rolls at a time for 3-4
minutes or until golden. Drain on
absorbent kitchen paper and serve
immediately.

Makes 20

These Spring Rolls are also
delicious made with beef,
chicken or prawns in place
of the pork.

Spring Rolls

ITALIAN MEATBALLS WITH EGG SAUCE

When shaping minced meat, dampen your hands and work on a lightly floured or dampened surface – this will prevent the mince from sticking to your hands and the surface. An egg added to mince mixtures binds them and makes them easier to shape.

$^1/_2$ cup/30 g/1 oz breadcrumbs, made from stale bread
$^1/_2$ cup/125 mL/4 fl oz milk
500 g/1 lb lean lamb mince
1 onion, finely chopped
pinch ground cloves
$^1/_2$ teaspoon ground cinnamon
1 egg
60 g/2 oz currants
60 g/2 oz toasted pine nuts
3 cups/750 mL/1$^1/_4$ pt chicken stock

EGG SAUCE
3 eggs
2 tablespoons water
3 tablespoons lemon juice
freshly ground black pepper

1   Place breadcrumbs in a bowl, pour milk over and set aside to soak for 5 minutes. Place mince in a large bowl, add breadcrumb mixture, onion, cloves, cinnamon, egg, currants and pine nuts, and mix to combine. Using wet hands roll mixture into small balls. Place meatballs on a plate lined with plastic food wrap and refrigerate for 15 minutes.

2   Place stock in a large frying pan and bring to the boil over a medium heat. Place meatballs in stock, bring back to the boil, then reduce heat and simmer for 30 minutes, turning meatballs occasionally. Using a slotted spoon, remove meatballs from stock and place on a warmed serving dish. Set aside and keep warm. Reserve 3 tablespoons stock to use in sauce.

3   To make sauce, place eggs, water and lemon juice in a saucepan and whisk to combine. Whisk in reserved hot stock and cook over a low heat, stirring constantly and without boiling for 3-4 minutes or until sauce thickens. Season to taste with black pepper and spoon over meatballs. Serve immediately.

Serves 4

For a quick version of this dish you can cook the meatballs in the microwave. When cooking in the microwave there is no need to use stock, simply place the meatballs in a round microwave-safe dish, cover with a lid or plastic food wrap and cook on HIGH (100%) for 7-10 minutes or until meatballs are cooked. Rearrange the meatballs after 5 minutes of cooking, placing the centre ones on the outside and the outside ones in the centre. Make the sauce as described above while the meatballs are cooking, using 3 tablespoons of vegetable cooking water in place of the stock.

Italian Meatballs with Egg Sauce

ENGLISH PORK PIES

Oven temperature
200°C, 400°F, Gas 6

4 cups/500 g/1 lb flour, sifted
1 tablespoon baking powder
250 g/8 oz lard, chopped
approximately 1¹/₂ cups/375 mL/12 fl oz
boiling water
1 egg, lightly beaten

PORK FILLING
500 g/1 lb lean pork fillet, minced
1 cup/60 g/2 oz breadcrumbs, made from
stale bread
1 small onion, grated
¹/₂ teaspoon ground coriander
¹/₄ teaspoon ground nutmeg
¹/₂ teaspoon dried thyme
¹/₄ teaspoon ground sage
1 egg, lightly beaten
2 tablespoons milk

1   To make filling, place pork, breadcrumbs, onion, coriander, nutmeg, thyme,
sage, egg and milk in a bowl and mix to
combine.

2   Place flour, baking powder and lard in
a food processor and process until mixture
resembles fine breadcrumbs. With
machine running, slowly add boiling
water to form a stiff dough. Transfer pastry
to a bowl, cover and set aside to rest for 30
minutes.

3   Divide pastry into two portions, one
portion two-thirds larger than the other.
Roll out the larger portion to 3 mm/¹/₈ in
thick and using a saucer as a guide cut out
six 15 cm/6 in circles. Use pastry circles to
line six ramekins. Spoon in filling.

4   Roll out remaining pastry to 3 mm/
¹/₈ in thick and cut out six 7.5 cm/3 in
circles. Brush rim of each pastry case with
a little water and top with pastry circles.

5   Crimp edges of pastry to seal, cut
steam vents in tops, brush with beaten
egg and bake for 40 minutes or until
golden brown.

Makes 6

Traditionally served cold,
pork pies are a substantial
addition to a packed lunch
or a delicious picnic treat. For
a casual weekend lunch,
you might like to serve a pork
pie as part of a Ploughman's
Lunch with a selection of
cheese, chutneys and
wholemeal rolls.

English Pork Pies

ROAST BEEF WITH YORKSHIRE PUDDINGS

Oven temperature
190°C, 375°F, Gas 5

This time plan will ensure that you get your roast dinner cooked and on the table without any fuss.

2 hours before serving
(Note: 2 hours for medium beef or 1³/4 hours before serving for rare beef)
Place meat on to cook for 30 minutes.
Make Horseradish Cream, cover and refrigerate until just prior to serving.

After 30 minutes of cooking
Add carrots, onions and parsnips to meat dish.

1 hour before serving
Place potatoes on to cook. Prepare a green vegetable of your choice, cover and refrigerate until ready to cook.

After 1 hour of cooking
Increase oven temperature to 220°C/425°F/Gas 7 and cook beef for 15 minutes longer for rare beef and 30 minutes longer for medium beef.

20 minutes before serving
Prepare Yorkshire Puddings.

15 minutes before serving
Cook Yorkshire Puddings. Make gravy and boil, steam or microwave prepared green vegetable.

---

2 kg/4 lb prime rib of beef on the bone
2 tablespoons vegetable oil
freshly ground black pepper
6 potatoes, halved
3 carrots, halved
6 onions, peeled
3 parsnips, halved
²/3 cup/170 mL/5¹/2 fl oz beef stock

YORKSHIRE PUDDINGS
³/4 cup/90 g/3 oz flour
1 egg, lightly beaten
¹/3 cup/90 mL/3 fl oz milk
¹/4 cup/60 mL/2 fl oz water
45 g/1¹/2 oz beef dripping

HORSERADISH CREAM
¹/2 cup/125 mL/4 fl oz cream (double)
1 tablespoon horseradish relish

1   Place beef in a flameproof dish, fat side up. Brush with 1 tablespoon oil, season to taste with black pepper and bake for 30 minutes.

2   Brush another baking dish with oil and heat in the oven. Add potatoes and bake for 1 hour or until potatoes are tender, turning halfway through cooking. Place carrots, onions and parsnips around beef and cook for 15 minutes then turn

---

vegetables over and cook for 15 minutes longer. Increase oven temperature to 220°C/425°F/Gas 7 and bake for 15 minutes longer for rare beef or 30 minutes longer for medium beef. Allow meat to rest in a warm place for 10-15 minutes before carving. Reserve baking dish and cooking juices.

3   To make Yorkshire Puddings, sift flour into a bowl and season to taste with black pepper. Place egg, milk and water in a bowl and whisk to combine. Make a well in the centre of the flour mixture, pour in egg mixture and beat slowly to incorporate wet ingredients. Place 1 teaspoon beef dripping in each of six muffin tins and heat in oven until dripping is sizzling. Divide pudding batter between muffin tins and cook at 220°C/425°F/Gas 7 for 10-15 minutes.

4   Skim fat off pan juices in reserved baking dish. Place dish on top of the stove and cook over a low heat, stirring to scrape up caramelised juices. Stir in stock, bring to simmering and simmer for 10 minutes or until sauce reduces and thickens. Pour into a gravy boat and set aside to keep warm.

5 To make Horseradish Cream, whip cream until soft peaks form. Fold in horseradish relish and season to taste with black pepper.

Serves 6

Roast Beef with Yorkshire Puddings

SAUSAGE ROLLS WITH CHILLI SAUCE

Oven temperature
200°C, 400°F, Gas 6

750 g/1¹/₂ lb sausage meat
3 eggs
freshly ground black pepper
750 g/1¹/₂ lb prepared puff pastry

CHILLI SAUCE
1 tablespoon vegetable oil
1 small onion, finely chopped
1 clove garlic, crushed
¹/₂ small red chilli, seeds removed and
finely chopped
¹/₄ cup/60 mL/2 fl oz lemon juice

remaining pastry. Divide sausage meat mixture into four portions and place filling down centre of each pastry strip.

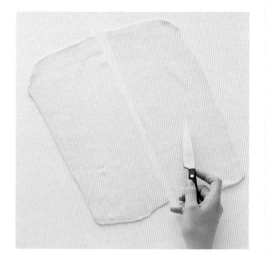

Instead of the Chilli Sauce you might like to serve the sausage rolls with tomato sauce or a selection of chutneys and relishes. Sausage rolls can also form the basis of a delicious meal. Cut the rolls into longer lengths – 10-15 cm/4-6 in is a good size – and serve one or two with salad and chutney for a complete meal.

1   To make sauce, heat oil in a small saucepan and cook onion, garlic and chilli over a medium heat for 3-4 minutes or until onion is soft. Remove pan from heat and stir in lemon juice.

2   Place sausage meat, 2 eggs and black pepper to taste in a bowl and mix to combine.

3   Roll out half the pastry to a rectangle 20 x 25 cm/8 x 10 in. Cut in half lengthwise to form two strips. Repeat with

4   Place remaining egg in a small bowl and whisk lightly. Brush edges of pastry strips with beaten egg and fold pastry over filling to form a roll. Cut each roll into 4 cm/1¹/₂ in lengths. Place rolls on lightly greased baking trays and bake for 20 minutes or until puffed and golden. Serve hot with Chilli Sauce for dipping.

Makes 40

Sausage Rolls with Chilli Sauce

PERFECT ROASTING

Roasting was originally done over an open fire where very large pieces of meat were turned over glowing embers until cooked through.

STEP-BY-STEP ROASTING

1 Preheat oven to 180°C/350°F/Gas 4.

2 Trim meat of excess fat and weigh meat to calculate cooking time.

3 Refer to Roasting Guide and calculate cooking time.

4 After the cooking time is completed, remove meat from the oven and set aside to stand for 10-15 minutes. Standing allows the juices to settle and makes carving easier.

ROASTING CUTS

BEEF: Fillet, Rump, Rib Roast, Sirloin, Fresh Silverside, Topside

VEAL: Leg, Loin, Rack, Shoulder

LAMB: Shoulder, Leg, Mid Loin, Rib Loin, Rack, Crown Roast

PORK: Leg, Loin, Shoulder (Hand or Spring)

There are several methods of roasting. The method you choose will depend on the cut of meat you wish to roast.

Dry heat roasting: The meat is first seared to seal in the juices and moisture, then oven-baked at a high temperature for a short period. This way of roasting is ideal for those who enjoy meat browned on the outside and rare in the centre. The more tender cuts of meat, such as beef fillets, boneless sirloin, rump, boneless rib and veal loin should be used for this method.

French roasting: The meat is cooked over a bed of chopped vegetables with stock or wine and covered for most of the cooking. The cover is removed towards the end of cooking to brown the meat. Rib roasts, topside, rolled briskets and fresh silverside are the most suitable cuts for this method.

Pot roasting: The more economical cuts of meat that would be tough if dry roasted are used for this method. The meat is first seared over a medium-high heat to seal in juices, then transferred to a covered roasting dish (Dutch oven) and cooked slowly in the oven, or simmered in a covered, large, deep, heavy-based saucepan on top of the stove. In both cases the lid must fit tightly. A small quantity of liquid and vegetables can be added if desired and basting is not required. Suitable cuts to use are topside, rolled brisket, thick flank, blade-bone and chuck.

ROASTING GUIDE

	Cooking Time per 500 g/1 lb	Internal Temperature
Rare	20-25 minutes	60°C/140°F
Medium	25-30 minutes	70°C/160°F
Well Done	30-35 minutes	75°C/170°F

Lamb: Irrespective of the weight, lamb rib loin, rack and crown roast are each only cooked for a total of 40-55 minutes at 200°C/400°F/Gas 6
Pork: Pork is always cooked to well done as in the chart above. For puffed, crisp crackling the first 20 minutes of cooking is at 250°C/500°F/Gas 9.

MEAT PURCHASING GUIDE

When purchasing meat, these tips will ensure that you purchase the best quality.

Allow 125 g/4 oz lean boneless meat per serve.

Lamb and beef should be bright red in colour with a fresh appearance. Pork should be pale-fleshed with a sweet smell, not slimy or bloody.

Select lean meat. If there is any fat it should be pale cream in colour.

In hot climates, take an insulated shopping bag with you to ensure meat remains cold until you get it home and refrigerate it.

MEAT STORAGE GUIDE

The following tips will ensure that the meat you purchase stays at its best for the longest possible time.

Fresh meat should be kept as dry as possible and should not sit in its own 'drip' during storage.

Store meat in the coldest part of the refrigerator. This will be the bottom shelf if your refrigerator does not have a special meat compartment.

The more cutting and preparation meat has had, the shorter the storage time – for example, mince has a shorter storage time than chops or steaks.

When storing meat in the refrigerator, place a stainless steel or plastic rack in a dish deep enough to catch any drip from the meat. Unwrap the meat and place on a rack in stacks of not more than three layers. Cover loosely with aluminium foil or waxed paper.

If your refrigerator has a special meat storage compartment, unwrap the meat, arrange in stacks of not more than three layers and cover meat loosely with aluminium foil or waxed paper.

If meat is to be used within two days of purchase, it can be left in its original wrapping. Store the package in the special meat compartment or the coldest part of the refrigerator.

Meat that has been kept in the refrigerator for two to three days will be more tender than meat cooked on the day of purchase, because the natural enzymes soften the muscle fibres.

Always store raw meat away from cooked meat or other cooked food. If your refrigerator does not have a special meat compartment, store the raw meat at the bottom of the refrigerator and the cooked meat at the top. Storing meat in this way prevents the raw meat from dripping onto the cooked meat and so lessens the likelihood of cross-contamination.

Raw and cooked meats both store well in the freezer, but as with any food to be frozen, it should be in good condition before freezing. To prepare raw meat for freezing, cut into portions required for a single occasion, such as a family meal. It is easier and more economical to take two packs out of the freezer for extra people than to cook too much through over-packing. If the meat is packed when you purchase it, remove it from the wrapping and repackage in freezer bags or suitable freezing containers.

Knowing a little about meat will help you understand why you grill a sirloin steak but casserole blade steak. Where the meat comes from on an animal determines how you are going to cook it. The tenderest cuts are from those areas that are the least exercised. The less tender cuts come from areas such as the shoulder or leg, which are in constant use whenever the animal moves. The guides to meat cuts and cooking techniques will help you understand meat better and how to cook it.

STORAGE GUIDE

Mince and sausages	2 days
Cubed beef, lamb and pork	3 days
Steaks, chops and cutlets	4 days
Roasting joints (with bone in)	3-5 days
Roasting joints (boned and rolled)	2-3 days
Corned beef and pickled pork	7 days

COOKING TECHNIQUES

Cooking techniques can be divided into two groups: dry heat and moist heat methods. The moist heat methods are pot roasting, casseroling, braising, stewing and simmering. The dry heat methods are pan-frying, stir-frying, crumb-frying, grilling, barbecuing and oven roasting. The following guide will help you choose the correct cut of meat for the cooking technique you wish to use.

POT ROAST

Beef: blade, brisket, chuck, round, fresh silverside, skirt, topside

Lamb: forequarter (shoulder), shank

Veal: shoulder/forequarter

CASSEROLE

Beef: blade, brisket, chuck, round, spareribs, shin, fresh silverside, skirt, topside

Lamb: best neck, forequarter (shoulder), neck chop, shank, shoulder chop

Veal: shoulder/forequarter chop and steak, neck chop, knuckle

Pork: diced pork, leg steak

BRAISE

Beef: blade, brisket, chuck, round, spareribs, shin, fresh silverside, skirt, topside

Lamb: best neck, forequarter (shoulder), neck chop, shank, shoulder chop

Veal: shoulder/forequarter chop and steak, neck chop, knuckle

Pork: leg steak

STEW

Beef: blade, brisket, chuck, round, spareribs, shin, fresh silverside, skirt, topside

Lamb: best neck, forequarter/shoulder and neck chop, shank

Veal: forequarter/shoulder chop and steak, neck chop, knuckle

Pork: diced pork

SIMMER

Beef: corned (salted) silverside, corned (salted) brisket

Pork: pickled pork

PAN-FRY OR PAN-COOK

Beef: blade, fillet, round (minute), rump, rib eye, spareribs, sirloin/T-bone

Lamb: best neck chop and cutlet, chump, leg and mid loin chop, loin chop and cutlet

Veal: cutlet, leg steak, loin chop, schnitzel (escalope)

Pork: butterfly (valentine) steak, cutlet, fillet, forequarter (sparerib) chop and steak, leg steak, loin chop and medallion steak, schnitzel (escalope)

STIR-FRY

Beef: fillet, round, rump, rib eye, topside, sirloin steak

Lamb: boneless leg, boneless shoulder, boneless mid loin, fillet

Pork: diced pork, schnitzel (escalope)

CRUMB-FRY

Beef: round (minute), topside steak

Lamb: best neck chop, rib loin cutlet

Veal: leg steak, schnitzel (escalope), loin chop, cutlet

Pork: schnitzel (escalope)

GRILL

Beef: fillet, rump, rib eye, spareribs, sirloin/T-bone

Lamb: best neck chop and cutlet, chump, forequarter, leg and mid loin chop, rib loin chop and cutlet, shoulder chop

Veal: leg steak, loin chop and cutlet

Pork: butterfly (valentine) steak, cutlet, fillet, forequarter (sparerib) chop and steak, leg steak, loin chop and medallion steak, schnitzel (escalope), spareribs

BARBECUE

Beef: fillet, rump, rib eye, spareribs, sirloin/T-bone steak

Lamb: chump, forequarter, leg, shoulder and mid loin chop, rib loin chop and cutlet

Veal: leg steak, loin chop and cutlet

Pork: boneless loin, butterfly (valentine) steak, cutlet, fillet, loin, forequarter (sparerib) chops and steak, leg steak, loin medallion steak, spareribs

OVEN ROAST

Beef: fillet, rump, rib roast, spareribs, sirloin, fresh silverside, topside

Lamb: breast, forequarter (shoulder), leg, mid loin, rib loin, rack, crown roast, shank

Veal: leg, loin, rack, shoulder/forequarter

Pork: fillet, loin, leg, boneless loin, schnitzel (escalope), shoulder (hand or spring), spareribs

---

Lean meat plays an important part in a balanced diet.

A 'balanced' diet is one which has a balance of the five food groups. The complex carbohydrates, fibre, vitamins and minerals from bread, cereals and other grain foods, fruit and vegetables; the high protein and calcium of dairy products, with very little added fat all help to create a balanced diet.

'The tenderest cuts of meat are from those areas of the animal that are the least exercised. The less tender cuts come from areas which are in constant use whenever the animal moves.'

Basic Lamb Cuts

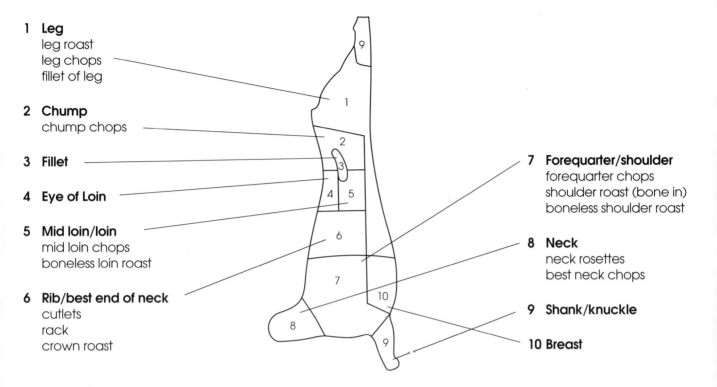

1 Leg
leg roast
leg chops
fillet of leg

2 Chump
chump chops

3 Fillet

4 Eye of Loin

5 Mid loin/loin
mid loin chops
boneless loin roast

6 Rib/best end of neck
cutlets
rack
crown roast

7 Forequarter/shoulder
forequarter chops
shoulder roast (bone in)
boneless shoulder roast

8 Neck
neck rosettes
best neck chops

9 Shank/knuckle

10 Breast

Basic Beef Cuts

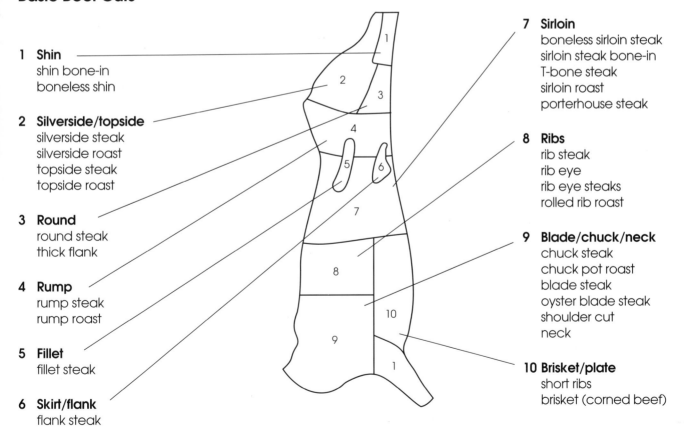

1 Shin
shin bone-in
boneless shin

2 Silverside/topside
silverside steak
silverside roast
topside steak
topside roast

3 Round
round steak
thick flank

4 Rump
rump steak
rump roast

5 Fillet
fillet steak

6 Skirt/flank
flank steak

7 Sirloin
boneless sirloin steak
sirloin steak bone-in
T-bone steak
sirloin roast
porterhouse steak

8 Ribs
rib steak
rib eye
rib eye steaks
rolled rib roast

9 Blade/chuck/neck
chuck steak
chuck pot roast
blade steak
oyster blade steak
shoulder cut
neck

10 Brisket/plate
short ribs
brisket (corned beef)

INDEX

PUBLISHER
Graham Billings

NZ Woman's Weekly
Food Editor: Robyn Martin

EDITORIAL
Managing Editor: Rachel Blackmore
Editorial Assistant: Ella Martin
Editorial Co-ordinator: Margaret Kelly
Recipe Development: Sheryle Eastwood, Lucy Kelly, Donna Hay,
Voula Maritzouridis, Anneka Mitchell, Penelope Peel, Belinda
Warn, Loukie Werle
Credits: Recipes pages 14, 64, 72 by June Budgen; pages 60, 61 by
Gordon Grimsdale; page 56 by Mary Norwak; page 50 by Louise
Steele © Merehurst Limited

COVER
Photography: Ashley Mackevicius
Styling: Wendy Berecry

PHOTOGRAPHY
Per Ericson, Paul Grater, Ashley Mackevicius, Harm Mol, Yanto
Noerianto, Andy Payne, Jon Stewart, Warren Webb

STYLING
Wendy Berecry, Belinda Clayton, Rosemary De Santis, Carolyn
Fienberg, Jacqui Hing, Michelle Gorry

DESIGN AND PRODUCTION
Manager: Sheridan Carter
Layout: Lulu Dougherty
Finished Art: Stephen Joseph
Design: Frank Pithers

Published by New Zealand Magazines Ltd
360 Dominion Road
Mount Eden, Auckland 3

Formatted by J.B. Fairfax Press Pty Ltd
A.C.N. 003 738 430
Output by Adtype, Sydney
Printed by Toppan Printing Co, Hong Kong

© J.B. Fairfax Press Pty Ltd, 1992
This book is copyright. No part may be reproduced or transmitted
without the written permission of the publisher. Enquiries should
be made in writing to the publisher.

Includes Index
ISBN 1 86343 054 7

Distributed by Medialine Holdings Ltd,
PO Box 100 243 North Shore Mail Centre,
Auckland
Ph: (09) 443 0250 Fax: (09) 443 0249